The Lakeside

Fire Memorial.

THE
LAKESIDE MEMORIAL

OF

THE BURNING OF CHICAGO,

A. D. 1871.

WITH ILLUSTRATIONS.

CHICAGO:
THE UNIVERSITY PUBLISHING CO.
1872.

Entered according to Act of Congress, in the year 1872, by

THE UNIVERSITY PUBLISHING COMPANY,

in the Office of the Librarian of Congress, at Washington.

ILLUSTRATIONS.

CHICAGO BEFORE THE FIRE.

FIRST HOUSE BUILT IN CHICAGO.
CHICAGO WATER WORKS.
FIELD, LEITER & CO.'S STORE.
CHAMBER OF COMMERCE.
BOOKSELLERS' ROW.
SHERMAN HOUSE.
PALMER HOUSE.
DRAKE AND FARWELL BLOCK.
COURT HOUSE.
NEW ENGLAND AND UNITY CHURCHES.
TRIBUNE BUILDING.

CONTENTS.

PART I.—BEFORE THE FIRE.

Chicago's History, Topography, and Architecture	*J. W. Foster.*	1
Our Trade and Commerce	*Charles Randolph.*	11
Our Æsthetical Development	*J. B. Runnion.*	18

PART II.—BURNING OF THE CITY.

Description of the Great Fire	*W. S. Walker.*	22
The Flight for Life	*H. R. Hobart.*	40

PART III.—AFTER THE FIRE.

The Burnt-Out People; What was Done for Them	*Andrew Shuman.*	43
Among the Ruins	*F. B. Wilkie.*	50
Reconstruction	*W. A. Croffut.*	53

PART IV.—THE LOSSES.

Real and Personal Property	*Elias Colbert.*	58
Commercial and Public Institutions	*Frank Gilbert.*	64
Religious and Educational Institutions	*E. O. Haven.*	71
Institutions of Art, Science, and Literature	*G. P. Upton.*	76

PART V.—THE FUTURE.

What Remains	*William Alvin Bartlett.*	82
New Chicago	*J. W. Foster.*	83

SUPPLEMENTARY.

The Fires of History	*Egbert Phelps.*	86
Science of the Northwestern Fires	*Elias Colbert.*	90
Political Economy of the Fire	*D. H. Wheeler.*	96

APPENDIX

Chicago and the Relief Committee	*Sydney Howard Gay.*	103

THE LAKESIDE MEMORIAL

OF

THE BURNING OF CHICAGO.

Part I.—BEFORE THE FIRE.

A GLANCE AT CHICAGO'S HISTORY—ITS TOPOGRAPHY AND ARCHITECTURE.

THE Conflagration of Chicago, October 8th and 9th, Anno Domini 1871, will form a memorable event in the future history not only of our own country but of the world; and therefore it is that we propose to embody in a permanent and accessible form for the benefit of the future annalist, the principal incidents connected with this tremendous event. This conflagration, in the amount of property consumed, is beyond the memory or example of ancient or modern times. Other great conflagrations, like those of London and of Moscow, swept away districts but imperfectly built, which subsequent enterprise beautified and adorned; but this conflagration wiped out the most substantially-built and beautifully-adorned portion of the city—structures, which in their solidity and in their architectural details commanded the admiration of every beholder.

There are men yet living and in the prime of manhood, who saw the site of Chicago when it was but a wet prairie. They have seen its fairest portions laid in waste; and they will live, very many of them, to see every trace of this waste obliterated. The same causes which led to the rapid growth of this city are still in operation; and this conflagration, disastrous as it was, will prove but a temporary check in the development of the great metropolis of the Northwest.

To comprehend the causes of the unprecedented growth of the city, and at the same time the magnitude of the disaster, it may not be deemed inopportune if we recur to her earlier history, and trace her progress, step by step, from small beginnings until she attained her late commanding position — the fourth city in point of population, and the third city in point of commercial importance, in the United States.

As early as 1672, the French Jesuits had explored and mapped the whole of Lake Superior, and the upper portion of Lake Michigan — then known as Lac des Illinois — as far south as Green Bay. They had established themselves at various points, among which were the Mission de Ste. Marie de Sault; Mission du St. Esprit, at La Pointe; Mission de St. Fr. Xavier, at the head of Green Bay; and the Mission of St. Ignace, at the outlet of Lake Michigan, nearly opposite Mackinac, on the north shore of the lake.* At that time the English colonists skirted the Atlantic Coast from Florida to Nova Scotia, without penetrating far in the interior. Elliot, in his missionary zeal, had explored only so far as Natick, six miles out of Boston; the Connecticut Valley was still unoccupied.

Among these Jesuit missionaries was James Marquette, a man of high culture but of meek and lowly disposition, whose name is indelibly engraven in the annals of the Northwest. He was attached to the Mission of St. Ignace. In his intercourse with the savage tribes, he had heard of the existence of a great river to the west, whose banks were bordered by vast prairies over which roamed countless herds of buffalo. On the 17th of May, 1673, accompanied by Joliet, with two canoes and five *voyageurs*, he embarked on a voyage to explore the great unknown river. Coasting along Green Bay to its head, then ascending the Fox River and descending the Wisconsin, one month after starting he beheld the mighty current of the Mississippi, on which he floated as far south as Arkansas. In returning, he paused at the mouth of the Illinois, and instead of proceeding on to the Wisconsin, ascended the latter stream, taking the Des Plaines branch, by which he passed by an easy portage to the Chicago River. Having reached Lake Michigan, he coasted along the west shore, and thus reached, after a canoe voyage of over 2,500 miles, the point of his embarkation.

So cordial had been the reception of the good father among the tribes inhabiting the valley of the Illinois, that he resolved to return and erect among them the standard of the Cross; and the next autumn (1674) he arranged to carry out his design. It was late in October when, with a canoe and two *voyageurs*, he embarked. Reaching the mouth of the Chicago River, he ascended that stream for about two leagues, where he built a hut and passed the winter. Game was abundant; and from his hut, buffalo, deer, and turkeys were shot. Originally of a frail constitution, this voyage had told fearfully upon the good father. Cold winds swept the lake, and notwithstanding the camp fires by night, his limbs were chilled. A hemorrhage, to which he was subject, returned with increased violence; and he predicted that this voyage would be his last. With the return of spring, his disease relented; when he descended to the Indian village below Ottawa, and there celebrated among the barbaric tribes the mysteries of the Christian faith. A few days after Easter, he returned to Lake Michigan, where he embarked for Mackinac, passing along the great sand-dunes which line its head, and thence along its eastern margin to where a small stream discharges itself into the great reservoir, south of the promontory known as the "Sleeping Bear." Marquette was so far debilitated that he stretched himself in the bottom of the canoe, and took little heed of what was passing. The warm breath of spring revived him not; and the song of birds fell listless upon his ears. Here he desired to land; and his attendants bore him tenderly to the shore, and raised over him a bark hut. He was aware that his time was come. Calmly he gave directions as to his mode of burial; craved the forgiveness

---

* To those interested in the early history of the Northwest, we commend the map entitled "Lac Svperievr et avtres lievx ou sont les Missions des Peres de la Compaigne de Iesvs comprises sovs le le nom Dovtaovacs," published at Paris, 1672.

of his companions, if in aught he had offended them; administered to them the sacrament of the Lord's Supper; and thanked God that he was permitted to die in the wilderness, a witness of His loving kindness. This event happened May 18, 1675.

Upon the banks of a stream which bears his name, they dug his grave and consigned his remains to the earth; but this was not to be his final resting-place. A year or two afterwards a party of Ottawas disinterred his remains, placed them in a birchen box, and conveyed them to St. Ignace, where, amid the priests, neophytes, and traders assembled to do them honor, they were consigned to a place beneath the floor of the chapel in which the good missionary had so often officiated.

Thus, then, Marquette was the first white occupant of Chicago, and that occupancy dates back nearly two hundred years ago. But for the calamity which has befallen her, it would be proper for Chicago, in 1873, to celebrate the two hundredth anniversary of her discovery, with bonfires and illuminations, and other evidences of public rejoicing; to go to St. Ignace and gather up and transport, with pious care, the ashes of Marquette, and erect over them the most elaborate mausoleum.*

La Salle followed in the footsteps of Marquette. Late in the fall of 1670, in four canoes, he passed the mouth of the Chicago River, circled the head of the lake, and landed at St. Joseph, on the opposite shore, whence he ascended that stream to what is now South Bend; and by the portage of the Kankakee, then called Theakiki, or Hankiki, he entered the Illinois Valley. In the fall of 1681, he passed by the Chicago portage *en route* to the Mississippi; and while this portage was repeatedly used by his followers, no permanent settlement was made at the mouth of the river.

By the treaty of Fontainbleau, in 1762, the vast territory east of the Mississippi passed into the possession of the British Government; and the Declaration of Independence, July 4, 1776, transferred this country to the dominion of the United States. In 1804, the Government established a military post at the mouth of the Chicago River, which was dignified by the name of Fort Dearborn; and a single company of infantry was deemed a sufficient garrison. In 1812, on the declaration of war, the Indians gathered about the fort and showed unmistakable signs of hostility. Captain Heald, then in command, foreseeing that his supplies might be cut off, and availing himself of discretionary orders, undertook to retreat with his little command to Detroit, three hundred miles distant; but he had proceeded less than two miles along the lake shore, when he was ambuscaded, and only three of his party escaped massacre.

In 1816, the fort was rebuilt and garrisoned by two companies of infantry. It was not until the close of the Black-Hawk War, in 1832, that the region of Northern Illinois and Southern Wisconsin was thrown open to settlement. Emigration soon began to flow in with an uninterrupted tide, which has continued up to the present hour. A hamlet clustered around Fort Dearborn, which took the name of Chicago. As late as 1837, flour was shipped from Ohio to supply the infant settlement; and in 1839 the first shipment of wheat, amounting to 1,678 bushels, was sent from this port, which is now the world's great market for breadstuffs and provisions. In 1840, Chicago contained a population of 4,470; in 1850, 28,269; in 1860, 109,263; in 1870, 298,977; and at the time of the fire hardly less than 350,000 souls.

* The name "Chicago" is a modified spelling of "Chekagou"; but this name was applied to a different stream from that of the Chicago River. In the map by Franquelin (1684) of "La Salle's Colony on the Illinois," the present Chicago River is called "Cheagoumeinan"; and "Chekagau" is applied to a small stream heading near the lake and entering the Des Plaines or "Peanghichia" River, above the debouchure of the Kankakee, and corresponding with Jackson Creek.

Nothing could have been more uninviting than the original site of the city. Ridges of shifting sands bordered the lake shore; while inland, and stretching beyond the range of vision, was a morass supporting a rank growth of blue-joint grass, with here and there a clump of jack oaks. Through this morass wound a sluggish river, only flushed by the spring and fall freshets; and adjacent to its banks were pools of water, which were the resort of wild fowl. The river's mouth was barred by shifting sands, but the bar once passed, deep water was found within. For a mile its course was east and west, when it branched into two forks, running northerly and southerly. This stream, so uninviting, forms the present harbor of Chicago, and separates the city into three divisions—the North, South, and West. The watershed between Lake Michigan and the Des-Plaines River—a tributary of the Illinois—was only eight feet in height; and during flood time, communication could

FIRST HOUSE BUILT IN CHICAGO—BY JOHN KINZIE, IN 1815, ON LAKE SHORE, NORTH OF RIVER.

be made in a canoe without disembarking. A well-marked channel can be traced, through which, up to comparatively recent times, a portion of the waters of Lake Michigan escaped to the Gulf of Mexico. Such were the topographical features of Chicago forty years ago. How wonderfully have they been transformed! The city commenced its growth upon the original surface; and so saturated was the soil with water, that cellars and basements were from necessity dispensed with. The streets in many places presented an oozy mass of mud, and here poles were thrust down bearing placards "no bottom." The more frequented thoroughfares were planked, and when driven over the planks were subjected to a churning motion which caused the ooze to spurt up through the crevices. The gutters at the sides were filled with stagnant water, whose surface was covered with a green scum, the appropriate nidus of the cholera and other pestilential diseases. So fatal were these pestilences, and so multifarious their forms, that medical terms were exhausted, and "canal" cholera was applied to designate a peculiar and fatal form of that disease; and the victims were left by the roadsides near Bridgeport, where they remained for a long time festering in the sun,—the citizens being afraid to approach the corpses, lest the disease be communicated to their persons, and thus propagated through the city.

The first impulse communicated to the growth of Chicago, was the passage, by the State Legislature, of an act, January 18th, 1825, for the construction of the Illinois and Michigan Canal; and in aid thereof, of the passage of an act of Congress, March 2d, 1827, granting to the State alternate sections of the public lands, embracing a zone of six miles wide on either side of the projected canal; but it was not until 1836 that the work was entered upon, nor was it completed until 1848.

In 1831, Cook County, embracing Chicago, was organized. In the spring of 1833, Congress made an appropriation of $30,000 for improving the harbor; and that same year a post office was established—John S. C. Hogan, who occupied a "variety store" on South Water street, being the first postmaster. The mail was brought weekly, on horseback, from Niles, Michigan. That same year witnessed the cession of all the lands in Northern Illinois, amounting to about 20,000,000 acres, by the Pottawotamies, who removed farther westward. Chicago was incorporated as a town by a nearly unanimous vote; and to show the number of voters, it may be said that twelve were in favor of and only one against the proposed measure.

In 1834, the poll list of citizens amounted to one hundred and eleven, and the amount of taxes reached forty-eight dollars and ninety cents; but this being inadequate for municipal purposes, the trustees resolved to borrow *sixty dollars* for the opening and improvement of streets. The next year, however, grown bolder by the success of the former loan, the treasurer, "on the faith of the president and trustees," was authorized to borrow $2,000, at a rate of interest not exceeding ten per cent., and payable in twelve months.

In 1837, Chicago became incorporated as a city, and William B. Ogden was chosen as its first mayor. From that time to the present, the history of the growth of the city becomes too complex to be traced, except in a comprehensive form. A series of public improvements was devised and executed, mainly under the direction of Mr. Chesbrough, as City Engineer, which made Chicago one of the pleasantest and healthiest cities in the Union. A system of sewage was established for underground drainage, which required that the original surface in many places be raised eight feet. This change of grade involved the necessity of raising many of the largest structures in those streets adjacent to the river. Such structures as the Tremont and Briggs Houses, the Marine Bank, and in fact entire blocks, were lifted up, with little or no interruption to business. Thus the city became thoroughly drained, the houses admitted of cellars, and the streets became dry and solid.

The mouth of the river, in 1816, according to the statement of Colonel Long, of the Topographical Engineers, was at Madison Street. It was a rippling stream, ten or fifteen yards wide, and only a few inches deep, flowing over a bed of sand. In the summer of 1833, the Government entered upon the improvement of the harbor, or rather commenced the construction of one. The north pier was extended a short distance lakeward, a lighthouse established, and an embankment thrown across the old channel to divert the water to the new course. An unusual freshet during the next spring tore out the sand and left a practicable channel into the river. The pier has from time to time been extended, until now it reaches a distance of about three thousand feet; and yet the problem of getting rid of the shifting sands thrown up by every northeaster, and leaving an open ship channel into the river, is far from being solved.

The river and its branches afford nearly fifteen miles of wharfage in the heart of the city; and the Dock Company, on the North Side, along the lake shore, have constructed works which add immensely to the harbor accommodations. The dock line is seven and one-half feet above low water mark. Thus, then, a tideless river and a nearly level plain afford almost unequalled facilities for receiving and distributing the immense freights which accumulate here.

To supply the city with pure water, Lake Michigan was resorted to as an unfailing reservoir. In the old works established on the North Side, the water was taken out near the shore. There were times when the current of the river, reeking with the sewage of the city, the offal of slaughter houses, and the slops of distilleries, was borne against this portion of the shore; and the drainage from the cemetery, populous with the dead, was also in this direction. Besides, during the winter, multitudes of small fishes would collect about the strainers and gain admission to the pipes, so that when the faucets at the houses were turned, out would come scores of minnows, some alive and some in various stages of decomposition. A violent northeaster would so roil the water that it became necessary to filter it. To obviate all these inconveniences, the novel, but as the result proved perfectly practicable, idea was conceived of drawing the water through a tunnel from the lake two miles distant from the shore. A

BUILDINGS OF THE CHICAGO WATER WORKS—ERECTED 1867.

shaft was sunk on the land side to the depth of twenty-six feet, and a "crib," pentagonal in form, forty feet in height and ninety-eight and one-half feet in diameter, was floated to the site in the lake and there anchored. It was then filled with stone and made to settle to its bed. An iron cylinder, nine feet in diameter, occupies the centre of the structure, and penetrates from the waterline to the depth of sixty-four feet, and thirty-one feet below the lake bed, where the tunnel commences. This is all the way excavated in a tough blue clay which offered no serious obstacles in the progress of the work. Its dimensions are five feet two inches in heighth, by five feet wide; and it is lined with two courses of brick laid in cement. Its capacity, under a head of two feet, is 19,000,000 gallons daily; under a head of eight feet, 38,000,000; and under a head of eighteen feet, 57,000,000. A tower, one hundred and thirty feet in height, contains an iron cylinder three feet in diameter, through which the water is forced by powerful machinery, and thence by its own pressure is distributed through the mains to the different parts of the city. Thus, at an expense of about two and one-half millions of dollars, Chicago has secured an ample supply of water, always pure, cool, and sparkling.

The river, as we have seen, was originally in the nature of a lagoon rather than a running stream. Into this river was discharged one-half of the sewage of the city, and upon its banks were numerous packing houses and distilleries, whose refuse added to the pestiferous contents. The color of its water varied all the way from inky blackness to rich chocolate brown; and the nasal organs had no difficulty in recognizing as many distinct stenches as Coleridge did in the River Rhine at Cologne. To remove this nuisance, which had become unbearable, the city, under authority of an act of the Legislature, passed February 16, 1865, proceeded on the plan of cutting down the canal for twenty-six miles to at least six feet below the low water-level of the lake. This plan was completed only last year, at a cost of about $3,000,000; and a current of pure lake water now flows through the city and discharges itself into the Mississippi, through the Des Plaines and Illinois rivers.

The intercourse between the three divisions of the city, up to a recent time, had been effected wholly by swing-bridges, which at intervals of two blocks spanned the river, whose average width is less than two hundred feet. These bridges were a serious impediment to navigation; and their almost continuous turning proved an equally serious impediment to vehicles and pedestrians. To obviate this inconvenience, a tunnel was constructed under the river at Washington street, arched for two hundred and ninety feet, by which an uninterrupted communication was established between the South and West Divisions. This tunnel proved so satisfactory that another tunnel was constructed under the river at La Salle Street, by which a similar communication was established between the North and South Divisions of the city.

The streets of Chicago were for the most part laid out on a liberal plan, which admitted of sidewalks ten feet wide and then of a grass plat in front of the residences for the planting of trees and shrubbery, with ample space for vehicles in the centre. Twenty years ago, to a stranger from an Eastern city they seemed unnecessarily wide; but it was fortunate that this plan had been adopted, for on the introduction of the horse-railway — the people's mode of conveyance — it was found that on either side of the track there was room for two teams to pass. In the improvement of the streets, the original surface was found to be ill-adapted to roadways: the soil was either sand or mud. Plank was first resorted to, and in 1854 twenty-seven miles had thus been laid; but it was found that with a mortar foundation and the churning process performed by each loaded vehicle in passing over, the planks soon formed a barrier to easy and safe locomotion. Macadamising was then resorted to; but the rocks in the neighborhood, being limestone, while they bedded themselves and served to form a solid foundation, crushed under the action of loaded teams and gave rise to intolerable clouds of dust. The same objection applied to cobble-stones. It was not until a system of drainage was established that a really permanent road-bed could be obtained. As far back as 1856, the Nicolson or wooden-block pavement was introduced; the cleanest, the neatest, and the least-noisy of all of the devices for sustaining the traffic of a great city.

The plat of the city with its several additions, up to 1870, occupied a space of six miles long and a little more than three miles broad. Along the lake shore, however, the houses stretched almost continuously from Hyde Park to Lake View, a distance of more than ten miles. In the area thus embraced, there were few vacant spaces dedicated to public use. To remedy this, the boundaries of the city were greatly enlarged; tracts of land were secured in the three divisions of the city for park purposes, which were connected together by boulevards; systematic plans of landscape gardening were vigorously entered upon; and the citizens anticipated the day, by no means remote, when these parks would become favorite places of resort, and form the pride and ornament of the city.

It is not surprising that a place built up so rapidly as Chicago had been, should present a somewhat incongruous appearance. The pineries of the north, which here found their principal distributing point, afforded materials for cheap and rapid construction. The accessions to the population of the city in the early stages of its growth exceeded each decade six fold, while in the latter stage it fell little short of three. The population thus flowing in required shelter, and landlord and tenant alike concurred, the one in erecting and the other in occupying, tenements of the most unsubstantial character. It is singular how airy these structures were. In the days of our boyhood, passed on the Atlantic Slope, we recollect that the getting together of the materials of a house and framing them, was a labor of no small magnitude. There were to be the sills, the studding, the joists, the braces, the rafters, and the ridge-pole, all of dimension timber; and when the whole was framed, the neighbors were called together, and with spike-poles they carried up the successive sides. To attend a " raising " was a notable event. But house-building in Chicago was a very different affair. With the exception of the sills, not a stick of timber entered into the construction which tasked the efforts of two men to carry. These structures received the very appropriate name of " balloon " houses; or, in other words, the greatest superficial contents with the least amount of material. As business increased and more massive and less inflammable structures were required, these houses were moved to the less populous districts; and the streets were constantly obstructed by these processions of old and ricketty tenements. The school section, in the heart of the city, was leased on short terms, and the lessees covered it with indifferent wooden buildings which could be moved off on the expiration of the leases. No policy could have been more short-sighted, so far as related to the substantial growth of the city—none so well calculated to bring in a meagre revenue. Hence, at an early day Chicago acquired the *sobriquet* of "Shantytown;" and well did she deserve that appellation. At the date of the fire there was no city in Christendom which contained such a vast mass of combustible materials. In European cities the term "shingle roof" is unknown, and partition walls of brick are universal in construction. Hence, a single apartment may be burned out, but the idea of a fire extending to a square is preposterous. Chicago, throughout her whole municipal history, had been cursed by a Council and a Board of Public Works who, through ignorance or self-will, were utterly indifferent to the ordinary precautions against wide-spread conflagrations. They placed no restrictions on the erection of two-story wooden buildings in the most valuable portions of the city, and outside of a limited area the taste or caprice of the landlord could be indulged without any control whatever. The cupola of the Court House, far above the reach of the water supply, was wood; and while the safes and vaults of every bank passed through the fiery ordeal comparatively unscathed, the records of every town lot and farm, and of every judicial decision, were consumed beyond the power of recognition. The Water Works, upon which the salvation of the city in such an exigency depended, were roofed with combustible materials, and no appliances were provided for putting out a fire. These events, the happening of which could have been prevented by ordinary precautions, argue a remissness on the part of the public authorities amounting to criminality.

In every city whose origin goes back to centuries, very many portions of it will be found to have been rebuilt. This process had been entered upon in Chicago, and the structures in the business part of the city, for the most part, were of enduring materials and almost faultless in architectural arrangement. Field, Leiter & Co.'s store was a more

FIELD, LEITER & CO.'S STORE.

imposing structure than Stewart's, on Broadway; the *Tribune* Building was one of the best-appointed newspaper offices in the world; the First National Bank Building, the Union Building, the Chamber of Commerce, the Merchant's Insurance Building, Drake's Block, Honore's Block, the Pacific Hotel, the Palmer House, the Bookseller's Row, the great station houses of the Michigan Southern and the Illinois Central Railroads, and other structures which might be cited, were models of architectural beauty. But the Court House, costly as a structure, was an architectural abortion; and every citizen, apart from the destruction of its contents, must rejoice that its walls are ruined beyond the power of restoration. The limestones from the line of the canal, the olive-tinted sandstones of Northern Ohio, and the red sandstones of Lake Superior, which had been employed in the facings of the better class of structures, gave to the buildings a warm and cheerful tint, not to be seen in any other city in America.

Many of the private residences on the North Side, and on Michigan and WabashAvenues, attracted attention by reason of their good taste and appropriate surroundings. Side by side with such structures were to be seen others which would fail to ornament an insignificant country village. With the best flagging stone on the line of the canal, and readily accessible to the city, yet in the burnt district there were nearly thirty miles of pine sidewalks which in the great conflagration became excellent conductors of flame, and forced the fleeing inhabitants to betake themselves to the middle of the streets. There was not, to our knowledge, a rod of brick pavement in the city. The tallest buildings, and of comparatively incombustible materials, were decorated with heavy wooden cornices, and roofed with shingles or a coal tar covering. The river, winding through the heart of the city, was lined with immense lumber-yards, coal-yards, planing-mills, sash-factories, and other combustible structures. Private greed, reflecting itself in the public authorities, looked only to the present, disregarding those precautionary measures which long ago were adopted by every considerable city in Christendom to guard against the effects of desolating fires. The cool-headed residents of Chicago, then, are far less inclined to attribute this overwhelming catastrophe to the judgment of God than to the folly of man. When human agency lays the train and fires the match, it evinces an overweening confidence in Divine Providence to expect that it shall intervene to prevent the explosion. Throughout the world's history, natural causes have been succeeded by natural events; and the destruction of Chicago was the legitimate result of the utter disregard of all precautionary measures to stay the progress of a destructive conflagration. When we shall have eliminated from this grand catastrophe all the elements chargeable to private greed and public incompetency, there will be left little or nothing to be carried to the account of Divine Providence. *J. W. Foster.*

OUR TRADE AND COMMERCE.
DEVELOPMENT OF CHICAGO IN WEALTH AND MATERIAL PROSPERITY.

THE growth of Chicago, in all that pertains to a great commercial metropolis, presents perhaps the most remarkable instance of rapid and uninterrupted progress of any city in the world, either in ancient or modern times. Going back to 1830, we find that the census of the United States gave Chicago a total population of only seventy souls; all, or nearly all, of whom were dependent upon the general government, which had established an Indian agency at this point. When it is remembered that this insignificant nucleus had grown within one generation to over three hundred and thirty-four thousand, as shown by a census taken but a few weeks prior to the great calamity, the question presses for solution — By what magic has this marvellous result been achieved? What peculiar combination of forces or circumstances has wrought a progress so wonderful and so entirely unparalleled?

While it cannot be denied that the city has drawn largely upon the best blood and most vigorous mental capacities, not only of our own country but also from foreign immigration, and to an extent that has made it a city representing by its people natives of almost every town and hamlet in this country and of Europe, thus consolidating into one homogeneous citizenship, the thought and enterprise of many and widely diversified intellects and educations, still all these advantages could not alone produce the results that have been manifest, and that have challenged the attention of the civilized world. In fact, this flood of emigration would not have set hitherward but for advantages of a permanent character that were apparent to the observing and inquiring mind. The not infrequent reference, both at home and abroad — sometimes in candor and sometimes in irony — to the spirit of enterprise and perseverance of the people of Chicago, has to some extent it may be feared done injustice to the peculiar situation and business facilities of the city. Men, however gifted in the diversified qualities of the successful and honorable merchant, cannot build up and establish trade where no trade is demanded or required to be done; and especially in this country men must seek the centres of business if they would command success as merchants: business will not to any great extent be diverted in quest of men. It is because Chicago has possessed remarkable advantages for the development of trade and commerce, that the remarkable results, now matters of history, have been attained.

Any review of the Trade and Commerce of Chicago, however hasty and imperfect, would be essentially incomplete without some reference to the basis of that trade, and the reasons that may be adduced for its rapid growth and development. First of all may be noted the broad expanse of matchless agricultural territory, dotted with farm-houses, villages, and cities, stretching hundreds of miles northward, westward, and southward, all more or less (and the major part of it entirely) dependent upon the city, both as a market for its surplus productions and a source of supply for those necessaries and luxuries that tend to make life enjoyable, and that are produced or manufactured in other portions of this or of foreign countries. But scarcely less important than supply and demand, because by it only can either exist, is the means of speedy transportation demanded by an extended commerce; and this, nature and art have supplied for Chicago to a degree unequalled by any interior city in the land: so that, with lines by water or by rail, the city has come to be a centre from which diverge in all directions ample avenues for conducting an almost limitless traffic, and through the influence of which the commerce of the city has been nourished and built up, and by means of which the great Northwest has become populous, and the hitherto cheerless prairie has been converted into a paradise of happiness, prosperity, and substantial wealth.

The early history of the Trade and Commerce of Chicago appears to have differed but little from that of most other Western settlements, consisting at first of a small Indian traffic, but gradually growing in proportions as civilization began to advance into the then almost trackless prairie. Early settlements in Illinois, as in other Western States, was confined almost exclusively to a proximity to such rivers as could be made available for transportation; hence what of trade there was, took the direction towards such markets as it could be floated to. Chicago was not one of these, for while nature had provided a grand and free highway for commerce from Chicago to the eastward, there were no avenues for it penetrating the interior, until they were created by the necessities of the situation. For the first eighteen years of its settlement, the only trade of Chicago was such as it drew from the immediately adjoining country, with a limited traffic in such commodities of actual and pressing necessity as were demanded by the settlers at a distance of one hundred miles. All farm products were sold, when sold at all, at comparatively low prices; and the entire product of a wagon-load of the most valuable available surplus of the farmer, when converted into such articles as he must buy, was scarcely sufficient to reward him for the time spent in effecting the exchange, to say nothing of the labor and capital employed upon his farm in its production. But notwithstanding the difficulties and embarrassments of both the producer and the merchant, the city had in 1848 increased in population to twenty thousand, and the taxable value of its real and personal estate, which in 1840 was less than one million of dollars, had risen to six million three hundred thousand dollars. Numerous wholesale establishments for the sale of all kinds of merchandise were in successsful operation, and already the trade in cereals had grown to respectable proportions. The attention of the State had at an early day been drawn to the advantages of connecting the waters of Lake Michigan with those of the Illinois River; and under liberal appropriations of the public lands by the general government in aid of the work, the construction of a canal from Chicago to La Salle, the head of steamboat navigation on the Illinois River, had been in progress for a number of years. After protracted delays, incident to the embarrassed financial condition of the State, this great work was completed, and opened for traffic in the spring of 1848. A new era in the commercial prosperity of the young city now dawned upon it; and with the rapid settling and development of the territory contiguous to this new line of transit, and the facilities it gave for communication with the whole Mississippi Valley, there sprang up a greatly enlarged trade, and an increased confidence in the stability and future greatness of the city. With the cheapened inland transportation, was inaugurated on a largely increased scale the trade in lumber, which has from then till now exhibited a uniformity of growth scarcely less marked and noticeable than that in breadstuffs and provisions. Nature has seemed to especially designate the banks of the little bayou on which man has built Chicago as a proper and necessary place for the exchange of commodities; for at this point, better than any other, can be united the different modes of transportation best adapted to the conveyance of those articles of commerce most largely produced or required by the people in whose interest the exchanges are made. Here meet for exchange the wheat, corn and stock of the farmer, and the product of the almost exhaustless forests of the peninsula of Michigan; the latter comparatively valueless but for the demand from the vast and fertile prairie lands, where there was scarce a native tree to break the desert-like monotony, and which in turn, but for the available supply of this building material, would be subject to an expense for a substitute that would greatly reduce their value. Thus each is dependent upon the other, and each by aid of the other has come to be thriving and prosperous — both meantime very materially aiding in the growth and advancement of the city through which the exchanges have been made.

The introduction of railroads, at a later but not distant day, was but the further development of transportation facilities, the necessity and advantages of which were made strikingly apparent by the acknowledged benefit resulting from the completion of the canal line. The first projected line — the original Galena and Chicago Union Railroad, now a part of the consolidated Chicago and Northwestern Railway, — was in its inception and during all its separate corporate existence under the control, in all respects, of citizens of Chicago; and although financial aid in its construction and equipment was sought and obtained of Eastern capitalists, it was always essentially a monument to the enterprise and faith of a few noble names of Chicago's early citizens. This line was, after hard struggles, opened to the Fox River, some forty miles from the city, in 1850; and although poorly equipped, it soon demonstrated the fact that although not furnishing as cheap a means of transit as water routes, it required but the construction of sufficient lines of railroad to make the great State of Illinois a very garden for production, and the home of a dense population. Other lines, which cannot here be alluded to in detail, were speedily projected and built; until, within a marvellously short space of time, the city found itself the centre of a system of railways diverging in every direction, all doing a prosperous and increasing business, eminently satisfactory to their share-holders, and conferring untold blessings upon not only the communities directly interested but the world at large. It may here be remarked, that although every principal line centring in Chicago has been built with special reference to Chicago's trade, and has brought with it increased commerce to the city, it has not been necessary to pledge the municipal credit or tax the body-politic one dollar in aid of their construction, nor has the accumulated capital of the citizens been drawn on to any great extent for their establishment. Chicago lines of railway have, in view of the wonderful past and prospective growth of their traffic, been so eminently profitable that capital from abroad has been ever ready to embark in their construction, sometimes even when her own citizens could not readily comprehend the necessity or prospective profit of the investment. The fact that no drain of this kind has been necessary, has left the citizens free to invest in mercantile or other enterprises of a local character, and has enabled them to meet municipal taxation for the extraordinary improvements necessary in a city requiring so much expenditure to make it convenient and enjoyable, without being oppressively burdened.

The subject of railroads may not properly be dismissed without a passing allusion to the great trans-continental lines built or in progress, and their effect on the commerce of the city. With the completion of the Union Pacific and Central Pacific roads, was demonstrated the fact that for the trade between the Atlantic Slope of the United States and the East Indies and China, this route presents advantages over every other, and especially so for the transportation of valuable freight, such as teas, silks, and the like; and a large and growing trade was at once inaugurated over the line, which has steadily increased, all or nearly all passing through or stopping in the city of Chicago. Our own merchants import largely *via* San Francisco, and find great satisfaction in the promptness with which they are enabled to receive their consignments, and the very favorable comparison they can institute between the present and the old way of receiving this class of goods. The finger of destiny to-day strongly points to Chicago as the great distributing-point for all Asiatic goods consumed in the Mississippi Valley. With the early completion of the Northern Pacific Railroad, a remarkably rich and inviting territory will be opened to the emigrant, and in addition very greatly increased facilities for the Pacific trade will result. That Chicago may, with its numerous favorable connections, reap great benefit therefrom, is not doubted by the careful observer of the course of trade. Already the trade with the mining regions of the Rocky Mountains is very large, and rapidly increasing. This of itself is of great value to our city, hardly appreciated by the mass of the people not directly interested or fully informed in regard to it.

Whatever may be said of the advantages to the Trade and Commerce of Chicago resulting from her other means of communication with the world, it must be admitted that her crowning glory as a commercial centre is the great highway provided by God himself for the free passage of her shipping on the great chain of lakes, one of the principal of which stretches its magnificent proportions before the eyes of her citizens, and by its pure and invigorating breezes brings health and joy to all within their influence. Without the aid of this means of transportation, her warehouses would become overburdened and choked, and her railroads could not be relieved of their enormous tonnage; in fact, but for this natural highway, no city would exist where now is so much of commercial life and varied industrial activity. But few, even of our commercial community, are fully aware of the extent of our lake commerce; and many will be surprised at the statement that our Custom House returns show very much the largest marine business of any in the country. The comparative statement of the different customs districts is not now at hand; but such was an official statement promulgated within the last few months. The number of entries of arrivals at our Custom House during the season of navigation for 1870, was 12,739 vessels; and of clearances during the same time, 12,433 vessels. The navigation of the lakes, though running through but about seven months of the year, is the grand safety-valve by which all rates of transportation eastward are regulated, and by means of it nearly all our lumber and vastly the largest share of our farm products are moved, the former to and the latter from the city.

Passing from theories of causes touching the wonderful growth of the Trade and Commerce of the city, and the means by which these have been developed, a brief reference to figures representing the facts in the past history of the city may not be inappropriate. Recognizing the agricultural interests of the West as the basis of all our commercial importance and prosperity, the trade in the products of the farm will be first alluded to. The first shipment of grain eastward from Chicago occurred in 1838, and consisted of seventy-eight bushels of wheat. This shipment was somewhat experimental in its character, and no more was forwarded until the next season. For several years subsequent, large quantities of flour were received in the city from New York State and Ohio, for local consumption; so that probably not until 1842 was there any balance of trade in favor of Chicago. In 1845 the shipments of wheat, and flour reduced to wheat (and in all the figures following flour will be treated as reduced to wheat), exceeded 1,000,000 bushels. In 1848, the year of the opening of the Illinois and Michigan Canal, the grain shipments exceeded 3,000,000 bushels. In 1852, when the influence of advancing lines of railroads began to be felt, the shipments reached near 6,000,000 bushels. From this time forward, the traffic assumed most remarkable proportions, reaching in 1856 an aggregate shipment of over 21,000,000 bushels; and in 1860, the year preceding the outbreak of civil war, the grain shipments of Chicago exceeded 31,000,000 bushels. During the next five years, the annual shipments ranged from 46,000,000 to 56,000,000 bushels. In 1866 it amounted to 65,486,323 bushels; since which time it has been somewhat less. In 1870 the shipments aggregated 54,745,903 bushels, the least since 1865 — the article of wheat in the grain being the largest of any previous year; while in corn, owing to a partial failure of the crop, the shipments had fallen to less than any of the previous ten years except 1864.

The prospect for the business of 1871, up to the time of Chicago's great disaster, was of a most flattering character, and promised for the year to be larger in breadstuffs than ever before. The shipments from January 1st to October 1st aggregated over 55,000,000 bushels, being fully 15,000,000 bushels in excess of that of the corresponding period in 1870; and the current daily receipts were larger than ever before at the same time in the season. The stocks of grain in store in the city at the time of the fire was about 6,500,000, being much the largest ever held here. A largely increased business was being conducted with Canada, and much more property had been purchased in the city for direct export to Europe than ever before. A line of substantial steamers adapted to the trade had been established between Chicago and Montreal, and had not only proved of great value to shippers, but were understood to have demonstrated the enterprise to be a wise financial investment. The enlargement of the Canadian canals, which is hoped for at an early day, will, it is believed, very greatly increase this trade, and will practically give to Chicago the advantages of a seaport, materially lessening the expenses of communication between producer and consumer.

Next in rank of importance to cereals, in the products of the farm that find a market in Chicago, may be noted the trade in live stock. No reliable record of receipts and shipments in this branch of trade appears to have been kept until 1857, though for several years previous a considerable business had been conducted; and as a point for the packing of both cattle and hogs, Chicago had taken a respectable rank as early as 1850. The receipts of cattle in 1857 amounted to 48,524 head, increasing the following year to 140,534; and thenceforward the growth of the trade was steady and rapid, until in 1870 the receipts reached 532,964 head, being near 130,000 in excess of the previous year. In the first nine months of 1871, the receipts were larger by nearly 40,000 than for the corresponding time in 1870 — indicating a large increase for the whole year. The receipts of live hogs, which in 1857 amounted to a little over 200,000, have increased much more rapidly, though with not the same regularity, as those of cattle. The receipts in 1870 amounted to 1,693,158 head, being only about 13,000 less than the greatest number ever received in one year. From January 1st to October 1st, 1871, the receipts were 1,393,274, being over 400,000 in excess of the corresponding time in 1870, — indicating a total of receipts for the current year very greatly larger than any previous year in the city's existence. A large number of hogs are sent to this market that are slaughtered in the interior — these aggregated in 1870 over 260,000. The larger portion of both cattle and hogs are sold here and shipped eastward, this being by far the largest shipping point in the country; but vast numbers of both are packed in the city and its suburbs. The packing of beef is carried on much less extensively than a few years since, the demand for the product having very greatly declined, and the business, what there is of it, being transferred to points nearer the feeding-grounds of cattle best fitted for this purpose. The packing of hogs, however, is conducted on a gigantic scale, the number packed at this point greatly overshadowing any other. The number packed at Chicago during the autumn and winter of 1870–'71, amounted to 919,197 head, against 500,066 head packed in Cincinnati, the point ranking next to Chicago in this line of business. In addition to the packing of the city, a very large amount of pork-product manufactured in the interior is marketed in the city, the receipts for 1870 aggregating over 40,000 barrels of pork and 52,000,000 pounds of other provisions, so that the provision trade of the city amounts to an enormous aggregate, and is increasing quite as fast as any other branch of its commerce. The articles of wool, seeds, butter, and in fact all kinds of farm produce, are largely marketed in Chicago; and the trade has assumed such proportions that in many of them large houses are exclusively engaged.

The trade in lumber in Chicago far exceeds that of any city in the land. In 1848 it amounted to 60,000,000 feet, in 1870 to over 1,000,000,000, and in all probability will considerably exceed this in 1871.

The trade in coal, salt, and many other leading articles, is in proportion to the demands of a country so dependent as is the Northwest for the importation of these articles.

Of the trade in general merchandise, including dry goods, groceries, hardware, drugs, paints, oils, boots and shoes, and clothing, it is safe to say that no city enjoys a larger or more satisfactory business in proportion to its population than does Chicago. Nothing could better illustrate the truth of this than the extent and magnificence of her temples of trade prior to the calamity which has laid the city in asnes. No city could boast of more extensive or elegant establishments for the transaction of business, or better adapted to the purposes for which they were constructed. In the dry goods trade, there were houses doing an annual business exceeded in only one city in the country; and in all branches of trade were merchants whose capacity for business, as well as the aggregate amount of their transactions, made them the peers of any either in the West or East.

In manufactures, Chicago was fast assuming a prominent place, although during her early years comparatively little attention was given to this subject, mainly owing to the fact that labor in other pursuits yielded a larger remuneration. For many years, however, the manufacture of agricultural implements, leather, highwines, and flour, have been most successfully conducted; and later, all kinds of machinery and castings, lead-pipe, shot, printing types and presses, furniture, boots and shoes, hats and caps, clothing, and many other articles, have been extensively manufactured; while large establishments for the manufacture of iron have sprung into being, and given employment to many hundreds of operatives. The amount of capital employed in manufactures in the city is probably not less than $40,000,000, with annual products amounting to at least $70,000,000, and furnishing means of support to perhaps 60,000 souls. No very reliable data, however, can be arrived at touching this important branch of the city's business, but it is believed the above may be regarded as approximately correct.

Intimately connected with the Trade and Commerce of the city is the question of Financial and Banking facilities; and in this regard probably no community has ever passed through so checkered an experience as Chicago. In the earlier days of the city it seems to have been the chosen theatre for financial adventurers, with little money and much assurance; though from the beginning very honorable exceptions may be noted to the general rule. Since the inauguration of the National Banking Law, however, a marked change has occurred; and at the present time no class of financial institutions rank superior to those of Chicago. There are seventeen banks doing business under the National Banking Law, and some ten to fifteen banking houses, representing a combined capital of nearly or quite $10,000,000. Universal confidence exists in the soundness and good management of these institutions, and their business is conducted with liberality, but with a wise discretion.

Such, briefly, has been the outlines of Chicago's history in Trade and Commerce, and such was her situation as regards business, present and prospective, when, in view of the past,— feeling cheerful, strong, and confident in contemplating the future, beaming with brilliant prospects and high hopes,— she is suddenly overtaken by the most dire financial calamity the world has

THE CHICAGO CHAMBER OF ERCE.

ever witnessed; in a day withering those hopes, laying in ashes her lofty and magnificent temples, both of worship and of trade, and utterly annihilating her treasures of beauty and of art; dividing the fortunes of her citizens by two, by four, by ten, or by an hundred, and some, alas! thrusting from wealth and luxury to actual penury and suffering. What wonder that for a moment her people stand appalled as they contemplate the awful wreck? But it will be only a moment: whilst some may find their burden greater than they can ever stagger under, others will gather together the fragments that remain, and with the aid of the outstretched helping hands from the four quarters of the globe, will repair the waste places, rebuild the levelled landmarks, and raise from the ashes of Chicago past, a city more grand, more substantial, and in every way more adapted to the needs of what the world has come to recognize as the necessities of Chicago future.

Charles Randolph.

OUR ÆSTHETICAL DEVELOPMENT.

IT is strange and sad to think of Chicago as among the things of the past. To remember what Chicago has accomplished and thereby judge what Chicago may accomplish; to look upon the massive walls that are already rising from the ruins; to watch the busy bees in great hives that have been thrown together to accommodate the trade which is as essential to the country as it is to Chicago; all this has something about it like the freshness of the wind that comes from across Lake Michigan, invigorating, exhilarating and health-giving. This is to partake of the true Chicago spirit which effaced the foot-tracks of the Indian with brick and mortar, and reared a magnificent city upon the sides of a crooked creek and in the marshes of the prairie. It is exciting and inspiring to contemplate the new growth; it is depressing and saddening to look back upon those things that can never be restored.

In a purely material sense it is partly true that

"One fire burns out another's burning,
One pain is lessen'd by another's anguish."

But in the products of genius, in the artistic and scientific hoardings of time — in the development of culture — the law of compensation seems to lose all its force. "Every day," said Robert Collyer in his lecture on "Our Loss and Gain,"— and it struck the writer as the most sorrowful sentiment of the evening's reflections, — " Every day we tread upon the cinders of things that we would have touched before with the greatest reverence." Could our old friend Colonel Foster, whose scientific attainments have received a national recognition, bring to life the treasures of the Historical Society or the wonders of the Academy of Science? The buildings may be restored as well as the Pacific Hotel; but the theory that absolute destruction is impossible becomes almost doubtful when we think of the paintings, the books, the manuscripts, the curiosities, the thousand and one things whose value was in their intangible contents, all converted into matter-of-fact carbon under the resistless torrent of one turbulent, awful sea of flame.

It is singular enough that a city of only thirty years' growth should now send the relics of its ruins to all parts of the world, but not more singular perhaps than that the brief span of a human generation should have served to develop the culture of a great metropolis. Those who doubt that Chicago had all this are not familiar with the story of its growth, and make the universal mistake, when speaking of Chicago, of comparing it with other communities that have had no longer existence. Its commercial life counting scarcely more than thirty years, its artistic life is, as a matter of course, still shorter. It is actually not more than ten years since the higher evidences of culture began to show themselves. Within that time, they have attained a prominence that is wonderful, not alone because of the briefness of the intervening space, but because they have forced a recognition in a community that has been regarded as purely mercantile in spirit. It used to be said that "Chicago is a good place for making money, but you want to go somewhere else to spend it;" it is not probable, however, that this sentiment has prevailed to any extent within the last three or four years.

It would be both foolish and wrong to hold that many of the characteristics of a Western city have not been retained, — among them a certain primitiveness of grammar, a broadness of expression, and a freedom of action that would frequently crop out to the infinite disgust of prim New England notions, and to the norror of "schoolmarm" rigidity of syntax and discipline. But along with all this, there were the variety of the metropolis, a cosmopolitanism in language and customs, an earnestness in the pursuit of art and culture, in strange contrast with the frigid and affected *connoisseur* of older cities, and a discrimination that was forming itself on the very best model of independence. A Chicago art criticism was apt to be somewhat confused in technique, but there has been no city to which artists would more gladly send their best productions, none other where they have been so certain of securing kind appreciation and patronage.

Perhaps the first genuine impulse given to art in Chicago was during the great Sanitary Fair, not more than eight years ago. Before that time, with a few individual exceptions, the auction sales of bedaubed canvas by the square foot were the sole and mortifying evidences of a kind of art taste "more honored in the breach than i' the observance." The exhibition and distribution of paintings in the Opera House lottery was certainly an illegitimate, but not the less useful, means of developing the sentiment of art, for it introduced new pleasures in this way, and had peculiar facilities for popularizing them. From this time on, true art became profitable; and the moment this point was reached there was a constant advance in the supply and a steady increase in the demand. The art stores soon doubled in number; four or five galleries were established; art-receptions became fashionable and gorgeous; some of the most famous modern pictures were attracted here; the private collections, of which there were three or four that would compare favorably with any in the country, increased and improved; a new and better taste was developed, and the time had come when mere ostentation in art had given way largely to its enjoyment. The merit of home productions grew in proportion. Men who had been forced to subsist upon cheap portraits and the coloring of photographs, found that such talents as they had would meet encouragement and remuneration in better work. The younger artists made their way to Europe for wider culture; the older formed themselves into an association for mutual improvement. The Academy of Design, after a life of only three or four years, had erected a handsome and commodious building; and after a number of superb collections, had, at the time of the fire, its gallery and its studios filled with choice and costly works.

In the love and appreciation of music, Chicago has advanced still more than in the love and appreciation of painting and sculpture. The taste had greater age, and, like good wine, was the better for it. While the public's estimate of artists is according to their merits, the artists' estimate of the public is according to its money. It was for this reason that Chicago has been, for many years, second only to New York in the favoritism of the musical *impressarii* and their combinations. Parepa, Nilsson, Kellogg, Theodore Thomas, along with their less famous companions and assistants, have always found so broad a sympathy and so liberal a patronage from Chicago people that, outside of any mercantile considerations — which, it must be confessed, go hand-in-hand with art now-a-days,— they have conceived and expressed the most sincere attachments to the city and its musical public. This gauge of art by the interest on dollars will attest the degree of culture in Chicago still further by the extent to which music had grown as a business. There have long been five or six of the largest piano and organ houses in the country, and, among numerous music-publishing firms, one at least compared in the amount of its productions to any other on the continent. The numerous representation of the German nationality among us has contributed largely to our musical culture. They have always had a great number of musical societies, and notably two — the Germania and Concordia — which have frequently given public exhibitions of their resources by the production of operas, symphonies, orchestral and choral concerts, which have contributed equal satisfaction and pleasure with many of the first-class entertainments coming from abroad. In the attraction of distinguishing musicians from other cities to a permanent home in Chicago; in the large number and superior quality of our church choirs; and in the excellence of purely amateur talent in society, Chicago's musical culture has been one in which the city and country might take a legitimate pride.

The drama has grown apace with the means for enjoying it,— not always in the right direction, but always far superior to all other Western cities. Four large theatres, two of which — Crosby's and McVicker's — presented a beauty and a convenience of arrangement unsurpassed anywhere, provided an incessant round of amusement, as various in its character as the tastes of a metropolis. For a time, the drama in Chicago sank under the incubus of meretricious performances, as did that of the whole country; but it had been more recently freed from this foulness, and was promising purer and more intellectual enjoyment. It was only some sixteen years ago that a gentleman, who has since been mayor of Chicago two successive terms, was playing three or four parts in one piece, was changing — a corpulent man himself — with an unreliable leading actor — a tall, thin man — in getting through with the character of the ferocious Richard, all in the same night,— an instance which curiously and humorously illustrates the primitiveness of the time. And yet, within this short lapse, gorgeous temples of the drama had been erected, and one or two of the managers were giving performances of the most chaste and admirable character. Such actors as Ristori, Janauschek, Booth, Jefferson, Mrs. Bowers, Adams, and others, played their most successful and remunerative engagements in Chicago, and attested their own confidence in the city which treated them so well by investing some of their large profits in its famous " real estate."

In literature, Chicago was making advances even beyond those in the fine arts. It had three of the finest and largest bookstores in the world, and sacrificed them at a loss of not less than a million of dollars. The bookstores on State Street, known as Booksellers' Row, comprised the three great firms of the Western News Co., S. C. Griggs & Co., and W. B. Keen & Cooke, and in the magnitude of the collections and in the variety of their contents, were unsurpassed, either in this country or on the Continent of Europe. Their combined sales reached $2,500,000 annually. In New York there is a division of the trade; and he who would seek imported books, or books of science and technology, or books of current literature, must resort to different establishments; but here were concentrated an assortment of books which embraced the whole circuits of knowledge. Leaving out the sites of the great public libraries, it may be said that nowhere on the surface of the globe, within an equal area, were condensed such treasures of knowledge as here. Chicago had long been as large a distributing centre for literature as for grain or lumber; it was fast becoming a most important productive point. The day is not more distant when the New York newspapers were sold in the streets of Chicago, and looked for as the only means for obtaining all the news, than was that when our only stage was of the backwoods description and drawn by four horses. Yet the fame of Chicago newspapers has already become world-wide. In circulation, profits, and influence, they are scarcely second to any in the United States. Their enterprise for news and their ability in editorial management are of a kind to satisfy the most exacting demands. The time had already come, too, when Chicago was beginning to make the proper distinction between the newspaper business and the art of literature.

BOOKSELLER'S ROW

THE LAKESIDE MONTHLY is one instance of the fact, of which there were many others. The publishing business was rapidly developing into excellence and profit. There were about one hundred publications in the city of a periodical nature, besides the increasing issue of books. Four public libraries of considerable size and worth, and probably fifty private libraries worthy of mention for extent, variety, costliness, or uniqueness, were contributing to our literary improvement.

All this fails to give even the briefest possible view of Chicago's development in culture before the fire. The material part is all gone, for the severest sufferers by that great conflagration, which rivers could not quench, were the institutions of music, the drama, literature, art and science. The rapid growth of this development has received a check which it may require years to throw off. Yet in the memory of what there was, there is great promise of what is to come. We shall never have to begin over again in the old, primitive fashion of half a generation ago; we shall begin where we left off, upon a surer and more healthful basis, with perhaps a slower but a more colossal growth. As to the abstract and spiritual quality of this development the burning of Chicago was as "uneffectual as the glow-worm to the matin."

J B R nnion.

Part II.—BURNING OF THE CITY.

DESCRIPTION OF THE GREAT FIRE.

A DESPICABLE combination of cow, kerosene, and baled hay, was responsible for it all.

The fact that early in the history of the blaze, and while its hot breath had only withered to their foundations a few of the rookeries in its immediate neighborhood, historical Mrs. Leary admitted that the fire had its origin in the manner popularly understood, is answer enough to the unreasonable doubts which have been thrown upon the story. Standing in the yard of her house—situated near the corner of De Koven and Jefferson Streets—this lady held forth exasperatingly to police, spectators curious, and reporters. Here it was that she implored maledictions dire upon the villainous bovine whose wretched hoofs had snuffed out her barn, and started the flames which were now licking savagely toward the river.

According to her statements in the early stages of the fire, and the reiterated assertions of her friends, she had taken an ordinary kerosene lamp, at about half-past nine o'clock in the evening of the fatal Sunday of October 8 in order to look after her ailing ruminant. Reaching the barn, she placed the light upon the flooring, and was on the point of putting a little feed into the manger when the cow sprawled out her heels in token of satisfaction.

An explosion; a sharp, brisk spreading of the burning oil; hay and straw eager to hand the flames up to the roof, in short, a barn on fire.

The woman hastened in feminine frenzy from the rickety structure to alarm the neighbors; but before the desired assistance could be laid hold upon there had been consummated an alliance of the riotous elements which only He who holdeth a world in the hollow of His hand could dissolve. It was an alliance of fire and tornado; a joining of hideous natural forces in a wild compact of destruction all the more appalling when we remember the contemptible means by which the union was effected. To be sure, in the sadly ludicrous fright of the succeeding days, this account of the beginning of the conflagration was stoutly denied by the wailing madame. But as a whimsical fright, lest herself and her lord might be compelled to foot the bill of some hundred millions of dollars' worth of incremated property, was acknowledged to be behind these denials, her first and less-biased asseverations must be accepted as the more honest ones.

Yet if the commencement of the giant conflagration was the result of pitifully insignificant causes, so were not the surrounding conditions by which the subsequent accumulation of horrors was entailed.

There had been a baking of earth, trees and dwellings, in the dry air of a rainless autumn, until everything had been cooked to the crisp, igniting point. There was a fire department, wearied with the labor of subduing a conflagration which, twenty hours before, had been thrown out as a skirmish line for the mighty hosts of flame that were to follow. Worst of all, a driving gale of wind was surging up from the southwest; a gale so steadily violent as to threaten disastrous hurricane, and to whip the waters of the lake into the white frenzy of a fearful storm. Against this combination of evils there was no force at hand strong enough to prevent the destruction of the sheds, dilapidated houses and shaky structures that comprised the "built up" portion of that part of the city in which the calamity was conceived. That the fire must be extensive in its reach, and completely sweep away the many wooden buildings in that quarter of the town, was obvious at the outset. But an earnest combat was, nevertheless, maintained against the enemy's encroachments. The three alarms, which in our municipal regulations denote a conflagration of unusual magnitude, and which summon all our engines to the scene of anxiety, had rung out inspiringly upon the night. The fire department had entered upon the customary battle with the flames, as sanguine as ever of being able to hold them within reasonable confines; for an hour every one believed that nothing more serious than another broad, blackened hole in the West Division would result.

But the drenchings from the engines, and the ripping away of fences and out-houses, availed nothing toward checking the progress of destruction. The narrow streets and alleys were beginning to overflow with people driven from their homes. The flames sullenly, but with an unequivocal certainty, were taking to themselves mightier proportions. They swung their lurid arms still further toward the river, brushing from existence every vestige of human work that lay in their path.

Soon the word began to be passed that the fire must reach the burnt district of the night before, ere any certain barricading of its march could be counted upon. A few only were recklessly prophetic enough to aver that its constantly augmenting wrath might endanger the safety of other sections of the city. Was there not a bare, smirched area of several blocks, left by the fierce blaze of the preceding night, along the river's edge? and who had ever heard of a conflagration powerful enough to stretch itself over such a space and threaten property beyond?

Such was the fair reasoning of those whose hearthstones were not being swiftly devastated. They saw only a magnificent spectacle; a spectacle already so grand as to dwarf from sight the minor episodes of humble families, wild with fright and the consciousness of suddenly inflicted poverty. But on swept the flames, and as they roared, snapped, and crackled along, in ever-growing fury, they seemed to be as little mindful of the attempts at their suppression as though men were but pigmies, and their impotent engines but the playthings of childhood.

A steady cutting away of human habitations; an atmosphere so rarefied by the intense heat as to cause the cooler air from beyond to rush in with whirlwind fantasies; all the space above dancing with swirling bits of burning timber, and alive with flakes of spinning fire; the thoroughfares filled with half-dressed, frantic women, dazed children, and powerless men, all burdened with dear mementos of the wasted home, and all pushing about in pitiful uncertainty to find the resting-place which was not to be found—this was the scene in the West Division as the battalions of fire held on in victorious array.

In something over one hour from

the commencement, the flames seized upon the planing mills, furniture shops, and other manufactories of similarly combustible material situated a little west of the river. From them it was only a vigorous stride to several of the largest elevators, and before midnight the conflagration had enwrapped more in value in its hot embrace than had ever before been sacrificed in our brief history.

It had demolished, leaving hardly one stone upon another, an extent of thickly settled country more than enough to form a city of respectable dimensions. It had left in blistering ruins the homes of thousands of poor people. It had destroyed many places of labor in which these people earned bread for themselves and families. It had blotted out of existence a large number of the most valuable manufacturing interests of the West; and it had blown from sight forever several enormous receptacles for the grain of the world.

The conflagration now hung upon the verge of the last night's work of ruin, and it was hoped by wearied fighters and victims of its anger that here it would rest. Beyond the open space of the old burnt area was the river, and beyond that were the proud stone edifices of the business heart of Chicago. Here, all thought, the fire-wraith would bow to circumstances too powerful for its fury. With tender care for the unfortunate ones, we would proceed to rebuild the devastated acres, and in a few months would show a pleased world, as we had so many, many times shown it in the past, how happy is Chicago in turning apparent evils into unmistakable blessings.

But suddenly there fell upon the sturdy complacency of the city an incubus so appalling that all its troubles in the past became insignificant. Hardly pausing to take new breath, the allied terrors of tempest and flame had leaped in fell carnival over into the South Division.

For a long time before the fire obtained its foothold in this part of the town, the savage blasts had been madly at work, dashing blazing emissaries from the melting structures in the West Division along the almost deserted ways of the business centre of the city. But with gravelled roofs, slate coverings, stone fronts, and alert watchmen, what was there of serious import to apprehend? Yet all this while Chicago was being rapidly converted into an enormous furnace. The materials were all ready for the blast, and the air of the furnace was already sucking through the huge flues of streets and avenues. The match only was wanting, and now that was applied.

The bridges and shipping in the river afforded a superb transit for the flames, and the crossings at Van Buren, Polk, and Adams Streets were soon frame-works of fire. From these, blazing in a raging wind, there was no lack of communication from the West to the South Side.

This latter was fired in two places, at a few minutes before one o'clock, on Monday morning; some three and a half hours after the origin of the conflagration in De Koven Street. The first of these was in a shed on the river bank, near Polk Street. This fire was extinguished with ease — although the structure was itself torn down, as the only method of checking the work of ruin.

At nearly the same time, the tar works belonging to the South Division Gas Manufactory, situated on Adams Street, near the Armory, were ignited. The firemen were well nigh exhausted; their engines were disabled, and the buildings upon which the fire had now fallen were of an excessively combustible nature.

In less than five minutes a square of buildings was in flames; the Gas-Works were attacked; the Armory, Chicago's principal police station, was toppling to the earth, and the legions of ruin had effected a terribly curious manœuvre, with a military exactitude savoring almost of reason. They divided their forces. One army of destruction marched swiftly toward the east, and the other sped away to the north. The first was soon across Fifth Avenue, and from thence moved upon the architectural grandeur of La Salle Street. The other dashed unchecked toward the no less noble structures that lined Monroe, Madison, and Washington Streets.

A double column of fiery devastation was abroad, and the core of one of the fairest cities on the face of the globe was doomed to yield to their imperious power.

Following the track of the eastward moving column of fire, or rather giving way reluctantly to its hot encroachments, the first great pang of sorrow came to the despairing spectators, when the flames stormed up to the Pacific Hotel.

This superb edifice, a caravansary built upon architectural precepts of the most artistic order, was six deep stories in height, and covered a full block of ground. The roof had just been placed upon it, and it was hoped that ere another year should dawn the establishment would be in readiness to receive the approval of nations, as the best hotel, all things considered, in America.

The sight of the billows of fire buffeting in, above, and around its superb lines, until it swayed and crashed in indignant protestation to the earth, was a proof against all imaginings that man had any power to cope with or mercy to hope from the terrific elements which had obtained control of Chicago. The intense heat was now continually creating new wind centres, by the rarefaction of the air, so that although the main course of the tempest was still toward the northeast, whirlwinds of fire were formed, which gave the conflagration abundant opportunities of beating up against the gale. Thus it was that almost at the same time the Pacific Hotel was consuming, the vast railway depot of the Michigan Southern road was burned.

The twin brawlers of fire and tornado, with their appetite sharpened by the feast among the cheaper buildings of the West Division, had gnawed to ragged crusts these two imposing edifices, and were now wild for a continuation of the repast. Down La Salle and across to Clark Street they rushed, swallowing in turn the Chamber of Commerce, Farwell Hall, and the rows upon rows of elegant stone and marble structures intervening.

Gunpowder was now called into use, and as it fulminated from street to street, substantial banking houses and the most ornate of trade palaces were hurled one by one into the air. Dark chasms were thus frequently opened before the path of flame in the lines of swiftly disappearing blocks, but all to no avail. A brief hesitancy, as if to gather new energy, and then a million sparks would dance over the abyss; an hundred tongues of fire would lap across the intervening space, and with melting shutters, cracking roof, and yielding stone, another block would be ablaze.

And now, while the heavens seemed to be metamorphosed into realms Plutonian, a curious study might have been made of the powerless people, around whom all this dire transformation was working. While a few men were laboring with Trojan-like energy to save something from the impending ruin, by far the larger proportion seemed inclined to assume the character of spectators. Men who in the face of ordinary conflagrations would have imperilled life and limb to preserve their own goods and those of their neighbors, stood calmly by, and passed quaint, terse jokes upon the excellence of the show. "It burns well;" "Chicago couldn't have even a fire on a half way scale;" "It lays over anything in history," is the embodiment of the comments that were bandied. It did appear as if the consoling balm of local importance and patriotism was dripping into every wounded fortune, and the fact that Chicago was bound to have a tip-top advertisement out of it, somewhat compensated for the swift entailing misery.

How a double column of blazing destruction started at right angles from the initial point of the South Division, at the tar works, has been noted. As they swayed along in search of further prey, these two columns threw out constant flanking lines of fire, filling in the streets, avenues, and alleys, in systematic order.

The northward moving line of ruin, chasing hotly up Market, Wells, Franklin and La Salle Streets, swallowed the cheaper buildings on the river ends of Jackson, Quincy, and Adams Streets; snuffed out the Nevada Hotel; baked to a crackling heat the stony approach to the east end of the world-famous Washington Street tunnel, and tottered from existence alike the dingy sailor boarding houses, the dens of dubious repute, and the erstwhile durable dimensions of the banking, commercial, and insurance houses that lay in its way. The coal yards, in which the winter's stores from Pennsylvania's exhaustless mine had just been heaped, were also enveloped in flame; and presently half a dozen or more of the grandest anthracite blazes of history were adding their glare to the illuminations of this new Eblis.

The destruction of the Nevada Hotel, one of the most successful of the second-rate hostelries, contributed no little to the uniqueness of the occasion. This establishment was overflowing with regular and transient boarders. Of the former, a large proportion were members of the dramatic profession, *attaches* of city journals, and clerks in prominent positions in the leading mercantile houses. The feminine portion of the histrionic delegation were particularly vehement in their expressions of disgust at being thus unceremoniously hustled from their comfortable quarters. It was vastly more dramatic than anything at which they had been called upon to assist, in their capacity of abstract chroniclers of the times, and they did not relish it at all.

The line of fire, with its flanking supports, which was eating toward the northeast, in a capricious spirit of mercy spared the Madison and Randolph Street bridges, over which ran the main city railways connecting all portions of the West Division with the South Side. A large five-story structure, just north of the last-named bridge, was also omitted, in either scorn or pity, and subsequently stood in majestic loneliness, the only unscathed edifice in the South Division, north of Harrison Street.

That thrifty thoroughfare of wholesale commerce, South Water Street, having been reached, the omnipotent angel of ruin who hovered over the city permitted the track of fire to turn again almost straight toward the lake. And now were swept away mammoth elevators, the Lumber Exchange, innumerable warehouses teeming with the products of the world. The wines of sunny France and Italy, the teas of China, the coffees of the Indies, and the staple viands of the Orient, were quickly tossed in steaming radiance to the zenith.

At the same time there perished the substantial accumulations of Lake Street, a business avenue which for gorgeous trade palaces and the value of their storied contents was abundantly capable of challenging any equal extent of thoroughfare in the land. Millions on millions of dollars, represented in the products of every quarter of the globe, fed the insatiable maw of the fire. At the lake end of the street there fell several excellent hotels, including the Massasoit, Adams, and Richmond, and that "good old inn," so revered by the appreciative travellers of the country, the Tremont House. The grand rendezvous of railway trains, that ganglion of tracks where centred the roads of half a dozen great companies, the Illinois Central Depot, was, in this quarter, the last seared monument of ruin left crumbling in hot protestation

DESCRIPTION OF THE GREAT FIRE.

at the unmerited fury of the tempest. Spinning along Randolph Street, the conflagration fed heartily upon the glories of the Briggs, Sherman, Metropolitan, and Matteson Hotels; upon stately business homes, Wood's Museum, and a miscellany of trade edifices that of themselves would have formed the heart of a small city.

The scenes at the destruction of the Sherman House were marvellously thrilling. Upwards of three hundred guests were lodged in the house. At the time the fire approached there were left in active charge only the night clerk and an assistant. The night clerk was not by any means the consequential hotel-employe of the period, but was a cool, energetic young man, with a remarkable fund of good sense.

THE SHERMAN HOUSE.

Of the three hundred guests, a large number were ladies, unaccompanied by male escort; and of these, five were so sick as to be confined to their beds. The night clerk, having sometime before secured the valuable papers of the place, proceeded, with his assistant, to arouse every sleeper in the house. The lone women were promptly conveyed to the lake shore, and there placed in charge of policemen who took them beyond reach of further danger. The sick ladies were placed in hacks by the omnipresent night clerk, and were being driven away, when, followed by his assistant, and seized with a terrible suspicion, he rushed after and stopped them. An instantaneous counting of thin, pallid faces, and lo! only *four* women were there. Five had certainly been recorded in the sick book of the house. It was then remembered that one poor lady was still remaining. Back into the now trembling structure dashed the two young men, one of them snatching from a fireman an axe as he passed. Up the stairways and through the smoke-reeking halls they groped, until the door desired was reached. Two lusty blows, and in it crashed, revealing the woman half raised in terror from the bed. It was the first intimation of the horrible danger that she had received. A word of explanation, and she had directed them to the closet where hung a dress and cloak of uncommonly heavy stuff. A pitcher and basin, fortunately full of water, served to drench these garments and the main quilt of the bed, and in them was quickly wrapped the invalid. Portions of the soaked clothing were then thrown over their own heads, and in a space of time hardly longer than it has taken to pen this episode, these heroes, than whom no braver shine upon the admired annals of the ages agone, had instinctively found their way through the familiar passages of the house, into the streets. When the writer saw them placing the fainting woman in a carriage, portions of their clothing had been burned into sieve-like perforations, and the hand of one was badly scorched. The hotel in a moment after folded itself to the glowing foundations, and was among the most complete wrecks of the night.

The Court House, an incongruous structure of mottled hues, and yet with fair pretensions to attention, stood alone in the centre of a large square, while the fire was tumbling to the pavement the stately edifices on two of the streets around it. That it must escape destruction was the generally-granted theory. But if the acres of flame could not lay fiery grip upon it, they could, aided by the ever-howling wind, send messengers of ruin hot and fierce upon its roof and dome. Soon a huge blazing timber flew against the dome. Instantaneously the entire upper portion of the building shot into flames. In the lower portion of the structure, which did disagreeable duty as the County Jail, there were confined, on every kind of criminal charge, more than one hundred and fifty prisoners. The jailer and an assistant turnkey, at the last moment compatible with safety, opened every cell and released each inmate. Happy in the brute consciousness that the ill wind which was showering extermination upon Chicago, had, with consistent ugliness, blown a precious boon to themselves, garroters, thieves, debtors, petty pilferers, and hardened murderers, shot off into the crowds and were seen no more.

Still "eating into the gale," the course of the conflagration pushed back upon itself until it had swept away the block upon which stood Hooley's Opera House, the Bryant and Chase Business College, the *Republican* office, and other hardly less noted structures. It had already cut out the northern part of this and the next adjoining block east, and was reaching in feverish anticipation of the revel in store for it at the St. James Hotel and Crosby's Opera House. In this latter building there were stored the instruments of three of the largest piano houses in the country, art treasures almost invaluable, and the works of decorators who had for several months been laboring lavishly at the beautifying of the auditorium. In the renovations of this auditorium the sum of $80,000 had just been expended, and the place, at the breaking out of the fire, stood complete, the finest temple of Thespis and Thalia in America. A luxury-loving public, who had anxiously read of its fair proportions, were to have pronounced upon its beauties on the night of its destruction. It was to have been formally re-dedicated on that same evening by the Thomas Orchestra, every seat having been sold a week before. Many of the more valuable paintings stored in this establishment were saved, but the number of dollars consumed in choice pictures alone stepped a long way into the thousands; while in the fall of the building and the perishing of its contents, there went down a valuation of over half a million.

The fire had now reached State Street, and was again working against the course of the gale, and pushing a trifle towards the south. This division of ruin, before reaching the corner occupied by Field, Leiter & Co.'s grand emporium, had laid in sweltering ashes the newspaper offices of the *Evening Post*, *Evening Mail*, *Staats Zeitung*, and *Chicago Times*, besides destroying the publishing places of many lesser places and miscellaneous publications. The office of the *Journal* was also soon added to the sad list, and then there remained not the home of any journal of importance save the superb structure belonging to the *Tribune* Company. The buildings on every corner around it had gone, and nothing but seething *debris* marked the sites of Reynolds Block, the Dearborn Theatre, and the store of Ross & Gossage, with the adjacent mammoth carpet warerooms belonging to other firms.

That even now a goodly portion of the business centre of the place must be left unharmed, was the almost universal theory. It was understood that the eastward-moving line of fire, which had broken from its companion column near the gas works, had spent its violence. There was then only the latter to subjugate, and with the advent of day surely this could be accomplished.

Remaining intact was the east side of Dearborn Street to the *Tribune* Building, and all of the fine property lying east of State until Randolph was reached.

But while this final glimmer of hope came to the hearts of the more understanding watchers of the fire, it was all too quickly shut out by the news that the flames had crossed into the North Division. This was at about four o'clock in the morning, a little before day-break.

Hardly had this announcement closed despairingly around the souls of those who had yet hoped against hope that something of value in Chicago might be saved, when the terrible tidings were whispered that the Water Works were in ruins, and that the only friend man had found among the elements in this his hour of necessity was taken from him.

There was now absolutely nothing left but to stand by and trace the path of accumulating devastation, biding the destroying angel's pleasure that the work of calamity should cease.

All along the east side of State Street, where stood some of the loftiest marts in the city, and on Wabash and Michigan Avenues, it was considered that comparative safety was insured. However, many of the dwellers on these last thoroughfares, as well as those persons who owned mercantile houses in the vicinity, took the precaution to remove large quantities of their more valuable goods to the open spaces of Dearborn Park, the base ball grounds, and the lake front. Here all was presumably safe, as even if the entire city burnt up, open ground could not be consumed.

And yet this very quarter was doomed to be the converging point for the two armies of fire that had parted from each other near the tar works. The march of the northward-striding line, with its slight but steady inflection to the east, has been shown. That which hurried toward the lake from the southern end of the Michigan Southern Depot had been slower in its labors, but none the less vindictively accurate in its work of ruin. It had swept from existence the shabbier structures of Third and Fourth Avenues, and had crept unrelentingly onward until De Haven Block and the towering grandeur of the Bigelow House and Honore's two massive marble buildings had fallen into ruin.

As the three noble structures last named reeled to the ground, the day was fully ushered in. But in the murky sunlight the ruin still held on; when it would halt, who should now dare to say?

From the Bigelow House to the Academy of Design was less than a block, only a bagatelle of a stride for the giant of conflagration that was abroad. Within the walls were husbanded some of the noblest works of art America could boast. Among these were a number of paintings which had just arrived in the city, and which were intended for display at the forthcoming fall exhibition; a new work by Bierstadt, valued at $15,000; dozens of precious pieces by leading artists of other cities; and the studios, with most of the contents, of more than twenty home painters. Rothermel's great canvas, "The Battle of Gettysburg," the property of the State of Pennsylvania, and the grandest historical picture in the country, was cut from its frame and saved. It has been conveyed within the precincts of the commonwealth to whom it came so near proving an irreclaimable and irreparable loss.

The Palmer Hotel, one of the youngest but already one of the most famous of our world-famed public houses, fell in at nearly the same time as the Academy.

Here, near the corner of State and Jackson Streets, and upon Wabash and Michigan Avenues, was now to be witnessed the frenzied stampede of thousands. The many were breaking in crazed haste to escape from the heat, and from the sight of the horrible scenes which had grown so terribly familiar. These swellers of the panic had in most cases secured portables of real or fancied value, and were madly, selfishly eager to take themselves, their families, and their chattels, beyond the reach of the insatiable fire demon's clutches. Some were on foot, staggering along under the weight of rich packs, and tugging at the hands of halting relatives. Others were piled, with stock from their stores, furniture, wives and children, into vehicles of every conceivable class, many of which had been hired at fabulous prices from their contemptible owners. But to add to the insanity of the scene, there were men seeking to struggle in the opposite direction. These were merchants who, living in the extreme South Division, and just learning of the night's disaster, were dashing in on foot and in their carriages, with a fierce determination to know if they too had been beggared while they slept.

The streets indicated were almost totally impassable, and so frantic was the struggle of teams and pedestrians that there were often complete dead-locks, during which not the least progress was made by any one. But these temporary stoppages in the retreat were insignificant in comparison to the frightful scenes which were constantly occurring in consequence of the choking of their roads and walks. Old men were thrown down and trampled upon; children were lost from their parents; and the parents were in many cases parted from each other, never to meet again. Women were knocked to the pavement by the rearing, madly-gallopping horses; and several authenticated cases of child-birth, in which both mother and infant were instantly killed, added their diabolical quota to this newest of pandemoniums.

And all the time the fire was leaving behind, in fantastic mould, the hot evidences of its withering strength; was reaching ever forward for more of splendor to level to the earth. By the continued blowing away of buildings in its path, as it prowled swiftly east on the line of Harrison Street, its course seemed to be diverted to the north again. In this was safety; for all that lay in the north must perish as it was now perishing, and so in that direction to keep the path of the burning storm was the only hope. Up again it worked, smiting down the blocks enclosed by State, Harrison, and Madison Streets, and Wabash Avenue. Here, as elsewhere, it fed its unglutted appetite with the richest of fare, and stately churches, beautiful dwellings, and proud trade palaces were alike devoured, walls, roof, contents and foundation stones.

Before daybreak the thieving horror had culminated in scenes of daring robbery unparalleled in the annals of any similar disaster. In fact, earlier in the history of the flames, the pilfering scoundrels had conducted operations with their usual craft and cunningness at evading observation. But as the night wore on, and the terrors aggregated into an intensity of misery, the thieves, amateur and professional, dropped all pretences at concealment and plied their knavish calling undaunted by any fears of immediate retribution. They would storm into stores, smash away at the the safes, and if, as was happily almost always the case, they failed to effect an opening, they would turn their attention to securing all of value from the stock that could conveniently be made away with, and then plough off in search of further booty. The promise of a share in the spoils gave them the assistance of rascally express-drivers, who stood with their wagons before the doors of stores and waited as composedly for a load of stolen property to be piled in as if they were receiving the honestly-acquired goods of the best man in the city. This use of the express-drivers was a double curse, in that it facilitated the abstracting of plunder, while it also took up the time of teams that might otherwise have been used by the merchants. The express-wagons once heaped with the loot, were driven pell-mell through the city, adding to tne dangers and the accidents of the surcharged streets, and the property was safely " cached " in the country.

Remonstrances on the part of the owner availed nothing. With no one to aid him in the preservation of his goods, or to assist in the apprehension of the villains, the merchant was compelled to stand quietly aside and see his establishment systematically cleaned out by the thieves, and then laid in ashes by the flames.

Several cases occurred in which the owners of stores came to the conclusion that if their places must go and nothing could be preserved, some decent people should have the benefits accruing therefrom. They accordingly threw open their stores and issued a loudly-delivered invitation to the crowd to hurry in and take away all they might be able to carry.

The scenes of robbery were not confined to the sacking of stores. Burglars would raid into the private dwellings that lay in the track of coming destruction, and snatch from cupboard, bureau, trunk, or mantle-tree, anything which their practiced senses told them would be of value. Interference was useless. The scoundrels hunted in squads, were inflamed with drink, and were alarmingly demonstrative in the flourishing of deadly weapons.

Sometimes women and children, and not infrequently men, would be stopped as they were bearing from their homes objects of especial worth, and the articles would be torn from their grasp by gangs of these wretches.

Reference has been made to the flow of liquor. Up to three or four o'clock in the morning there was a surprisingly small percentage of intoxicated persons to be counted in any quarter. But as the physical and mental exhaustion pressed heavier, and as the dull horror began to settle upon each soul that perhaps not one stone might be left standing upon another, the inexplicable seeking for an assuage of trouble in potent alcohol followed. Saloon-keepers rolled barrels of the poison into the street, and the owners of great liquor houses threw open their doors to the overwrought and haggard populace. Men drank then whose lips had never before been crossed by alcohol; while those who had hitherto tasted of its Lethe-draughts only on rare occasions, now guzzled like veteran soakers.

This was a new accession to the woe of the event. There were hardened women reeling through the crowds, howling ribald songs; coarse men were breaking forth with leering jokes and maudlin blasphemy; women of the highest culture tossing down glasses of raw whiskey; ladies with cinder and tear-begrimed faces, pressing the cups with jewelled fingers; while of rich and poor, well-bred and boors, the high and the lowly, there were few who did not appear to have been seized with the idea that tired nature must finally succumb unless the friendly stimulant was used. All were not intoxicated; all were not drinkers. There were probably thousands who found in the taste of wine, or stronger fluids, the nerving to new deeds of heroism and quiet bravery. But the drunken phase was a terribly prominent one, and one that entailed an awful addition to the woes of the conflagration.

At about eight o'clock on Monday morning, the enormous branch of the fire which had cut its way eastward, with a pronounced deflection to the north, and which a few hours before was erroneously supposed to have been checked, almost joined its resistless power to its companion branch from which it had been cleft at the gasworks. This junction was not, however, quite formed, owing to a fitful change in the artificial wind-currents which sent the line of flame that had destroyed the Bigelow and Palmer Houses, Honore and other blocks, a little to the westward, sealing the fate of McVicker's Theatre building and the block adjoining the *Tribune* Building on the south.

Although taught by the cruel lessons of the night that it was hoping against hope to think to preserve any of the buildings on which the fire demon had turned his baleful eye, there were still a few undaunted workers ready to engage in another combat with the foe. Earlier in the night, a huge tar cauldron that had been left a few days before by some roofers in front of McVicker's, had been laid hold of by several young men and dragged where it should be incapable of mischief. Much of the combustibles stored in the alleys was also removed, and then all was done that could be done, save to hope. At the *Tribune* Building, men for a time occupied the roof, sweeping away coals, while another force was alert for similar duty at the doorways and windows.

But, with exultant derision at all the puny efforts put forth to cheat it of its prey, the conflagration closed hopelessly around this block. McVicker's naturally gave way first. The *Tribune* Building was not long in following, and although at first offering a stubborn front, was eventually left a haughty but none the less complete wreck. It was a wreck doubly assured, in that although presenting for days afterward a more imposing display as a ruin than most of its contemporaries, it was still so insecure as to lead to the death of men who trusted to its stability in seeking to repair it.

The line of bookstores comprising the celebrated "Booksellers' Row," a handsomer congregation of houses devoted to the dissemination of universal literature than existed in such friendly neighborhood in any city upon the globe, perished at nearly the same time as the edifices whose fate has just been described.

A little further to the north was the elegant architectural pile occupied as a dry goods store by Field, Leiter & Co. During the previous hours, as the waves of conflagration were beating savagely around it, copious floodings of water had been emptied over every portion of this structure. Its internal economy included an extensive system of pipes, conduits, and hose, connected with the water mains under ground. It was through the aid of these that the drenching was kept up; and had it not been for the sad failing of the Water Works in the North Division, the unexampled furnace blasts which were howling on nearly every side of it could not have materially affected this building. Smaller structures, including the Cobb Library house, were demolished with powder in hope of saving Field, Leiter & Co.'s building. But the same weary story of unavailing labor, of hasty firing and speedy destruction, that had been repeated over and over again, ensued here. At the final surrender of this edifice, the four walls of which rolled in dismal thunder into the basement at nearly the same instant, there was seen a strangely attractive gulf of glowing iron pillars, braces, and columns, shimmering in the white and red heat of the flames.

And now, with its forces joined to the companion column of ruin which had swept away so much of wealth and beauty elsewhere, and had sent a twin-demon of fire carousing in devastating revelry through the North Side, the battalions of flame that had just accomplished the destruction of the Field, Leiter & Co.'s building, moved on toward the lake front. From Harrison Street down a portion of State Street and Wabash Avenue, a few blocks of fine buildings had thus far been spared, while a great desert of smouldering waste was stretched far into the west and north.

The allied army of flame threw out its broad arms in the direction of the lake — the huge branches of fire sometimes streaming, borne upon the pinions of the gale, for whole blocks. Along the lake front and upon the base ball grounds were huddled thousands of people; and, as has been noticed, there were also stacked in that neighborhood the richest of wares from adjacent stores, and the rarest of furniture and fittings from private houses. The goods had here been stored under the care of trusty watchers, as a spot perfectly secure from destruction, while the vast crowds of homeless people had gradually centred here for the same reason.

Suddenly it seemed that the fire had for the first time discovered this assemblage of humanity and property. The flames had feasted already upon all that was rich and rare in commerce, art, and literature; had been gorged with the proud wonders of architecture, and had tasted the sweet morsel of roasting, suffocating men, women, and children. And yet here had ventured to congregate a crowd of human beings with a few of the more precious of their stores, as if to defy, in one place at least, the omnipotent fury.

The conflagration swung its broad tongues of fire for acres, lapping greedily at the grand structures in the lower ends of Wabash and Michigan Avenues, and fairly pinning the terrified concourse between two enormous lines of fire which were steadily compressing together from their right-angle divergence. The fire fattened upon what it fed, and grew momentarily larger, lustier, fiercer. It sent off a rain of brands, burning timbers, and huge sparks, and flecked the air with myriads of blazing bits of material over the heads of the affrighted thousands.

A panic as complete as any that had reigned in other portions of the city followed. The crowd leaped instinctively for the south, and shot along the strip of park by the lake in bare time to escape the hurricane of fire that was seeking to cut off their retreat at the foot of Washington Street. The accumulated goods took fire, and in a few minutes, with the fences, seats, and pavilion of the base ball grounds, were withered to ashes, and the ashes swirled out into the wailing waters of the lake.

Nothing remained for the fire to finish the plumb line of ruin which seemed to have been drawn along Harrison Street, but to turn back and chop away at the few beautiful blocks which were standing in a mournful fringe on Michigan and a portion of Wabash Avenues. These were several majestic churches, the imposing proportions of Terrace Row, and the numerous costly dwellings of men who a little time before might have been rated as merchant princes, but who were now alternating between a moderate competence and stark beggary. Several buildings were blown up, but it was the same tale over again. The flames would bridge the gap, and the ruin would sweep on as before.

Terrace Row was the last to yield.

It was a beautiful edifice, solidly constructed, and in the face of any common fire would have refused to submit. But after burning some three hours, during which time a large share of the superb equipments of the many distinguished homes were transferred to a safe place, the last wall of the building reeled to the earth; and in the South Division there remained north of Harrison Street only the blocks of buildings east of Wabash Avenue and south of Congress Street, the Wabash Avenue Methodist Church, now converted into a Post Office, standing on the southeast corner of the Avenue and Harrison Street, the five-story building already named at the east end of Randolph Street bridge, and the Illinois Central Elevator just north of the once magnificent depot of the company.

Although the destruction proper did not commence until shortly before six o'clock in the North Division, the work of ruin in that section of the city antedated this time in that a part of Lill's Brewery and the Water Works were consumed between four and five o'clock.

That the Water Works should have burned at so early a period, and before the main body of the flames had reached the North Side at all, has given rise to a deal of very natural wonderment. The fact of this deplorable phenomenon taking place pointed the arguments and gave redoubled force to the assertions of those who were determined that incendiaries were responsible for the whole city's incremation. There is no reasonable ground, and never was, for declaring that the firing of the Water Works was due to malice. For hours the roaring wind had borne all the way from the perishing buildings of the West and South Divisions blazing messengers of ruin in almost a direct course to the Water Works. That many of the cheaper buildings in the North Division did not take fire an hundred times was much more of a miracle than that one or two edifices were prematurely consumed. The fact that it was the Water Works that burned so early of course attracted particular attention, whereas had a score of insignificant sheds elsewhere blazed up at one time, it would have been laid to the same causes that led to the destruction of the brewery shed, with its companion calamity.

The air of the North Division, at two o'clock in the morning, was alive with burning, flying wood; and these whirling brands, dropping upon a shed connected with Lill's Brewery, shot the flimsy structure into a sharp blaze. From here the destruction was partially extended to the Water Works, as the attention of the engineer and his assistant was drawn away from its proper post, during which time a large shower of larger sparks than usual came pelting upon the roof of a shed close to the building in their charge. With the terrible gale which raged all the higher near the open front of the lake, it was impossible to stay the course of destruction; and soon the works were so badly injured as to check the working of the engines, and Chicago was without water at the moment when water was to her the one great thing needful.

The full work of burning out the North Division, as before stated, began at a short time before six o'clock, or a full two hours after the immolation of the pumping works had stopped the supply of water.

No less than four different spots have been designated as the precise point at which the destruction of the North Side began. All of the assertions are to the effect that the bridges were the conductors of the flames, although a few claim in addition that the shipping assisted in ferrying the fire across. The most reliable statements, and those which are numerically the strongest, assert that Rush Street bridge passed the flames over the river, and that once across they danced briskly up to the Galena Elevator, which was soon enveloped in fire.

Here, as in other parts of the city, was witnessed the strange spectacle of

DESCRIPTION OF THE GREAT FIRE.   35

the wind driving the body of flame in one direction while flankers of fire ate along almost against the gale. The conflagration crept quickly west in an almost due line along North Water, Kinzie, and Illinois Streets, until a solid barrier of flame two blocks in thickness was created from the lake to the river.

Every bridge on the main channel had by this time been destroyed, and when the end of La Salle Street was reached, the heat created around its narrow orifice a suction so vehement as to pull through flames from the great warehouses on its southern extremity. The massive blocks of stone forming the towers were shattered, while the heavy masonry approaches and winding steps at either end were split, seamed, and cracked, and in some instances were burned to powder. As a proof that the flames were sucked through the greater portion of the tunnel, it was found, several days after, when the rubbish had been cleared from its openings and transit once more made convenient, that the wooden wainscotting, extending waist-high along its interior, had been calcined, and was at the northern end in perfect charcoal condition.

The wall of flame once built over the river terminus of the North Side, its previous tactics were abandoned, and it held straight on until it had brushed the North Division from existence. It was an enormous phalanx of fire from two to five blocks in thickness, extending from one side of the Division to the other. To seek to pass through it and strike for the main channel of the river was as far from possibility as it would have been to walk through a smelting furnace a thousand fold hotter than ever was made, to scale the heavens, or to ford the lake. There was time to think of doing but one thing, and that one thing was to flee. Those who yielded to the instinct of self-preservation and rushed far to the northward as fast as quaking limbs would bear them, unmindful of friends, of relatives, or of precious mementos of their disappearing homes, were alone certain of safety.

The lighter structures with which this Division abounded gave the magnificently hideous legions of flame a glorious opportunity of keeping their lurid ranks unshaken, and the wall of fire never presented an opening until the wooded confines of the extreme northern part of the Division were attained. Sometimes a specially obdurate structure, as the Cathedral of the Holy Name, or the monster breweries of Sands, Huck, and others, would resist for a brief moment, when a slight gap would show on the face of the flaming barrier. But ere the rear of the column could pass, the ruin would be as complete as if the building had disappeared from view at the first attack.

From the expressions of some of the more intelligent of those who were making a push for the open country to the far north, the sight must have possessed a certain terrible grandeur that was not to be observed in the detached work of devastation either in the West or the South Divisions. Here it was straightforward and unrelenting as destiny. It was a phalanx of fire extending as far as the eye could reach to the east and the west. Behind it none could see, and as to what might be its solid thickness the stricken ones before it had no means of determining. To them it appeared as if the world itself must be on fire, and that the flames were swiftly following their course around the entire globe.

The conflagration in this Division was more unforgiving than elsewhere, for here it spared only the merest fragment. In the other two portions of the city it had been satisfied with eating away a monstrous cavity on one side of the river, and with cutting the head from the body of the second section of the town. But in the North it seemed to have determined that not a house should be left to boast itself luckier or more irresistible than its humbled fellows. How one dwelling was saved in the midst of the surrounding desolation, and how a little slice on the northwest corner of the Division was also spared, form two of the most peculiarly interesting incidents of the whole record of ruin.

The story of the preservation of Mahlon D. Ogden's residence, a large and comfortable frame structure situated almost in the heart of the North Side, has already been fully given by the unwearying workers of the daily press. Briefly reproduced, the truth and marvel of the affair is that the building was in the middle of a block, all the other lots of which formed its elegant garden. On the streets upon its four sides were not many large buildings; while just as the fire approached it from the southwest there was a slight lull in the fury of the wind. This allowed the flames to shoot straighter into the air, and before the storm had again bent them forward in search of further fuel, the structures upon which they were immediately feeding had been reduced to ashes, and a break made in the terrible wall of fire. The exertions of Mr. Ogden and his family in covering the roof and walls of the house with carpets, quilts, and blankets, which were kept constantly wet with water from a cistern which happened to be in his place, also aided materially in the salvation of their home, which was the only unharmed building for miles. But the brief cessation of the tempest's violence was, after all, the chief cause of this singular exception, as even the fence which was on the windward side of the dwelling was only slightly scorched.

Precisely how the corner of the North Division, lying adjacent to the river, in the extreme northwest, was saved, has not, it is believed, ever been made public.

At about four o'clock in the afternoon of the fatal Monday, Mr. Samuel Ellis, an officer of the city detective force, who will be favorably remembered as Dixon's associate in the working up of the celebrated Ziegenmeyer case, formed a small company of his friends into a preventive squad. Ellis and the friends whom he summoned to his assistance were living in a long, handsome block on Lincoln Avenue, between Sophia and Webster Avenues. At the corner of this block, and intervening in the course of the rapidly approaching flames, between the block and the street, was a small frame house belonging to a widow lady. Divining at once that if this corner house could be saved perhaps the block in which he lived might also be spared, Detective Ellis directed and aided his little company with remarkable sagacity. There was a cistern in the yard full of water, and here was an invaluable ally able to preserve the widow's house, if understandingly used, and if mortal forethought and energy could preserve anything in this most unsparing of conflagrations. The roof of the building, as well as doorways and window-sills, were covered quickly with a deep coating of sand which was soaked with water. Quilts, carpets, and blankets were next procured, and the cottage was fairly swathed in them, and again the friendly water was called in until they were thoroughly drenched. The fences contiguous were ripped down, and the wooden sidewalks torn up.

By this time the huge sheet of fire was close upon the busy workers, and they were forced to rush back and trust that their efforts might not have been in vain, as had been the no less arduous labors of thousands in other parts of Chicago. The fire reached sharply over and licked around the enshrouded house, but before it could dry the coverings of wet sand and cloth, the force of its strength in that quarter was spent, and a fresh gust of the tempest sent it slanting toward the lake.

The corner house was saved; so also was the adjacent block, and by this means a fragment of the North Division enough to form of itself a village, closely settled, of a very respectable magnitude.

Cheated of its purpose in ploughing

away every vestige of the North Division, the fire drove wickedly onward in the direction of Lincoln Park and Wright's Grove, and ceased not in its work of ruin until Fullerton Avenue, the extreme northern limit of the city, was attained.

Here, with nothing further upon which it could riot, it at last died away into the second night of its carouse; and, just as a long-prayed-for rain came pattering coolly down, the Chicago fire passed into history.

By nightfall of Monday, a great number of refugees had collected in the cemetery at the south end of Lincoln Park, and many had endeavored to dispose themselves as comfortably as possible until the light of another morning should enable them make their final escape. But the fire-wraith hesitated not at the pollution of the quiet homes of the dead, and was soon curling the leaves and snapping the brush at the cemetery's entrance. Another stampede was all that was left to the heart-sick multitude of living ones, who had vainly thought to catch a few hours of fitful rest upon the graves of the sleepers below, whom even this tyrant conflagration could not touch. Out from the cemetery swarmed the stricken ones, and into the park, from which they were again routed by the untiring pursuit of the wind and the flames.

The only rest was upon the chilly margin of the lake and the bleak wilderness of the open prairies. The edge of the lake was lined with its dreary quota of those who, twenty-four hours before, had gone to rest in happy homes at the close of a Sabbath differing to them from no other Sabbath which had preceded it, but which was the dividing line between prosperity and utter ruin.

Only a few of the incidents of the conflagration can be added to those previously given.

Mr. J. H. McVicker, proprietor of McVicker's Theatre, going into his building by a side door from the alley, just as the flames had fully closed upon the structure, was driven back by the heat and the smoke. But on reaching the open alley, he was placed in a still more dangerous plight, being caught in one of the howling currents of air, created by the heat, which were whirling through in an exactly opposite direction from the main course of the gale. This brought a shower of sparks and burning bits of timber upon him, and before he could escape a tongue of fire was swaying through the alley. Throwing himself upon his hands and knees, he crawled out to the next street as rapidly as possible; but when he reached a place of comparative safety, he found himself almost blinded by the heat and the smoke, so that he did not regain the full use of his eyes for weeks.

At the burning of the Oriental Block on La Salle Street, opposite the Chamber of Commerce, a man remained in the third story long after the building had fired, composedly carrying his goods to a window and dropping them out, when they were thrown into an express wagon by his partner and two friends. A rope was all the while dangling from the window; and when his companions and the crowd implored him to desist from his work and leave the doomed building, he would shout back, pointing to the cord, "That is my stairway, now don't you fret for me!" At length, after every staircase in the house was in flames, and escape by the ordinary avenues was impossible, he came to the window with some books and money from the safe which he had opened. Throwing the books to his friends, he quietly shoved the money into his bosom and proceeded to crawl out and let himself to the ground by the rope, hand over hand in the most approved sailor fashion. He was within a few feet of the pavement, when the flames, breaking through a window from an apartment under which he had been at work, burned the rope instantly to a snapping condition. It parted, and the brave fellow tumbled upon his side, dislocating his shoulder. He scrambled up and was lifted into the wagon by his friends, muttering between his shut teeth as he patted the money in his breast with his sound arm, "Three thousand dollars all safe! I guess that 'll settle the doctor's bills."

In the West Division, just before the Van Buren Street bridge, the steam fire engine "Fred Gund" had been stationed, and with but a short stretch of hose, and a perfect salamander of a pipeman, was endeavoring to do its little share toward checking the further advance of the foe. But soon the heat grew too savage for even the case-hardened firemen. The hose pipe from which the water was still shooting was leaned upon a fence, and, as the horses had been taken away, the pipe and engine men were forced sadly to relinquish their beloved "tub," and sorrowfully retire across the bridge. But there stood the "Fred Gund," with steam up, jumping to its work as merrily as ever, while a little way in front the stream was sputtering as briskly into the flames as though it was playing only upon the flickering shed of a reporter's "incipient fire," or was engaged in the friendly rivalry of a peaceful "muster" with some brother engine. The steamer, rattling in every joint, was heard shaking and blowing long after the flames had shut it from sight.

The burning of the Van Buren Street bridge immediately after, led to a peculiarly picturesque scene. As the fire approached its western end, the men whose duty it was to swing the structure, warned everybody to leave, by an energetic tug at the bell. They then applied the turn-lever, and, giving two or three hasty spins as a starter, darted to the south side and squeezed through to the street. The bridge, by the impulse thus given, slowly swung open, but not in time to prevent the western end from catching fire. In a moment it was a grand, fantastic frame-work of flames, and in the eddies of the tempest and the artificial currents of heat was kept swinging to and fro, a huge specimen of grotesque pyrotechnics, which but for the overshadowing importance of preceding and subsequent events would have furnished a charming theme for description by skilled reportorial pens.

The old perverse absurdity, so common in seasons of great excitement, which leads frantic humanity to fritter away the priceless moments in the perpetration of deliberate stupidities, had a thousand illustrations during the fire. Those who threw the looking glass out of the window, and laboriously tugged the feather bed down stairs, had innumerable representatives and counterparts. A prominent legal gentleman, whose office was in Reynolds' Block, was guilty of solemnly enwrapping a wash basin, pitcher, spittoon, and two imitation bronze statuettes, in a table-spread, and dropping them over the banister of the twisting stairway at the northern end of the building, after which he shuffled back and groped around until he had loaded his arms with substantial law books, which he enthusiastically bore in safety to the sidewalk.

The Thomas Orchestra, stopping at the Sherman House, met with adventures numerous. The more interesting ones, in the present connection, were that nearly every member grasped a linen coat, a pipe, a piece of portable furniture, or something of like importance, and bore it proudly into the street, leaving the musical instruments with which their fame and daily bread were to be earned, behind them. The accomplished Miss Marie Krebs, the *pianiste* of the party, emerged from the blazing pile in a condition of complete tranquillity. She had covered her person with a dingy morning wrapper, and had secured, at the last instant, about half the score of one of Strauss' waltzes, and she clung to that bit of sheet music with all the persistency of a woman who had saved her most sacred heirloom from destruction.

Mention has been made of the fierce rain of sparks that fell in the South and North Divisions, borne from the burning edifices of the West Side, long before the fire had reached the South Branch of the river. These sparks pelted down in a shower so sharp that it is a marvel the igniting of the other two divisions was so long delayed. As an evidence of the intensity of this blazing rain, it is recalled that the clothing of those in the streets and of the watchers upon the house tops were often burned full of holes, and in some instances were actually started into flame.

Another incident must close the list here given, although the remembrance of others is well-nigh interminable, and the temptation to recount them is difficult to resist.

At the destruction of the St. James Hotel, a gentleman, whose wife was bed-ridden at that establishment after a wearying search commenced an hour before, had secured the services of a hackman and his team for the lady's removal. The driver had demanded the outrageous sum of sixty dollars, and not only refused to abate a penny from that amount, but was not inclined to stop and dicker, preferring to drive around the city, sure of meeting somebody whose necessities would ensure him as much, if not more, than his modest demand. The gentleman, however, was only too glad to obtain a comfortable conveyance at any figure; and the bargain was closed, and the carriage driven to the hotel. The lady was then brought down to the door, and a break was made in the crowd upon the walk to allow of her being carried to the hack.

Just at this moment up ran the proprietor of a leading jewelry house, whose richly-stored building was but a few blocks away. Justice to him requires it be observed that he did not understand the *status* of affairs. He only saw an unemployed carriage. Breathlessly addressing the tender-hearted driver, he said:

"Here, my man! I've tried for two hours to get hold of an express wagon, and it's no use. I can make your hack do as well, I guess. I'll give you a five hundred dollar note to let me pack it full of my goods, as many times as I can between now and the time the fire gets to the store."

"Good enough," answered the humanitarian of a Jehu. "Five hundred dollars is the word," and slamming the hack door, he was on the point of leaping upon the box and driving away. A howl of anger went up from the throng upon the walk, but save for the presence of a certain trio of young men it is more than probable that the poor invalid would never have been removed, unless carried in the arms of her husband and friends.

This trio was made up of three Bohemians of the press, who, having given their valuable benediction to the office in which they had been employed, as it crashed to the ground, had concluded that a choice quantity of time was now left upon their hands in which to achieve bright acts of benevolence. Here was an unmistakable opening. A dozen quick words passed between them, and in a twinkling their *coup* was effected.

Two of them stepped up to the faithless knight of the whip, and ere his astounded senses could exactly grasp the situation, they had lifted him over the curbstone into the middle of the street, and were applying a judicious kicking to his perturbed physique The other burst open the door of the hack, motioned to the husband of the sick lady, and in half the time it will take to read this had seen them comfortably stowed in the carriage, received their instructions as to their destination, mounted the box, seized the reins, and starting at a tearing pace around the corner, was soon out of sight.

William S. Walker.

THE FLIGHT FOR LIFE.

HOW can pen describe the scene — the wild flight of half a cityfull of people from their burning homes! The awful experience is written with a pen of fire in the memories of those who participated in the flame-urged exodus, but the aggregate of fear, of bewilderment, of despair, of mental agony, of physical pain, can never be adequately pictured; nor can there be properly recorded the courage, the self-possession, the generosity, the mutual helpfulness which also marked the astonishing scene.

The exodus began on Sunday evening in a little cluster of humble dwellings, and increased in volume and area and rapidity, as a mountain stream swells into a resistless river, until it had swept its scores of thousands of unhappy victims out to the great sea of the prairie and left them to perish or float with the tide. At first the few poor wretches whose humble abodes the fire was actually closing upon, picked up their effects and hurried them out to friendly doors close at hand, while the indifferent spectators looked on, strong in faith of the power of steam and iron over fire, and thoughtless of any danger to their own homes. But as an hour went on, the area of the flames had increased to a fearful degree, and hundreds of idle spectators had been converted into panic-stricken householders, frantically engaged in saving their own effects and transferring them to the places of safety which still abounded. The fire crossed the river and laid its devouring hand upon a broad margin of the South Division, while its pillar of flame and smoke led the way far ahead and began to waken the entire city to a sense of its peril. But still the scene to those whose homes were being consumed had only the ordinary terrors of a city fire, for there were still thousands of hands ready to assist in saving the occupants and their effects, vehicles were easily obtained, and places of shelter were close at hand.

But the fire rushed on into the heart of the city, and then the full horrors began. Then the instinct of self-preservation, that makes men blind and deaf to the needs of others, took possession of the frantic multitude. The whole city seemed doomed, and men began to look out only for themselves. The fiend had licked up the vile haunts along the river and on to Wells and Griswold Streets and similar neighborhoods, and sent the shameless women and half drunken men flying for their lives, no one caring for them. It had reached the solid business blocks, and their thousands of lodgers were added to the frantic throng. Then it knocked furiously at the many doors in the great hotels, and the terrified guests — strangers in a strange city — rushed about in the mazes of the halls, dragging great trunks and brandishing carpet-bags, seeking the doors, and disappearing into the pandemonium without. Meantime, too, it had swept over to the great residence avenues and served its writ of ejectment on the rich men's mansions, and reduced their delicately nurtured occupants to the unaristocratic level of the now shelterless inmates of tenement houses — a panic-stricken, heterogeneous mob of men, women, and children, fleeing from the fire.

Then, when the consternation became general, the demon Selfishness, that is within us all, asserted his supremacy, and the scene took on its worst features. The inmates of threatened houses with wild haste conveyed such valuables as they could into the streets, and then found the work of salvation scarcely begun. Assistance could not be obtained for love or for money, each man being busy with his own losses, or heedless of individual needs in viewing the immensity of the ruin. And so those who had nothing to lose too often stood by and saw men and women and children distractedly trying to save their treasures, and gave no helping hand; or, worse yet, drew near only to pillage. Vehicles rose to an astonishing value, and hackmen and express-drivers were eagerly offered fabulous sums to convey person and property to safety. Fifty and one hundred dollars a load was a common reward. The streets were filled with an indescribable mass of fugitives forcing their way through the chaos. The dust rolled in stifling clouds in their faces, often making it impossible to see a wagon's length ahead, and the falling fire-brands burned the clothing of the fugitives and maddened the horses, so that danger to life and limb was added to the other terrors. As the night waned — a night that needed no candle, lit as it was for miles around with the lurid light of the fire,— the flames kept crowding back, up the streets and avenues of the South Division, and the morning found them still eating their way, almost against the wind, devouring other palaces of trade and other dwellings with their luxurious furniture, their costly works of art, their countless treasures, hallowed by association, and possessing values that money cannot represent. Lake Park, fronting Michigan Avenue, was sought by thousands as a place of refuge, and millions of dollars' worth of goods were deposited there only to be devoured by the falling fire, while their owners fled for their lives. When at length the southward progress of the conflagration had been stayed at the irregular line formed by Congress, Harrison, and Polk Streets, the population of the South Division for miles above were still frantically moving their effects southward, or had gathered together such as they could possibly hope to save, and stood ready to fly with them when the destruction could not be averted.

But the scene in the South Division, where the fire moved comparatively slowly, and, over a large area, ate its way eastward and southward against the wind, giving gradual warning of its approach, was almost tame compared with the spectacle in the North Division. There the inhabitants were fleeing *with* the wind — the wind increased to a tornado by the terrible heat, and whirling the fire-brands before it like chaff. If the fire *walked* through the solid blocks of brick and stone in the business centre, it *ran* through the rows of frame structures that constituted the most of that part of the town. On the one hand was the lake, on the other the river with its scattered bridges quickly choked and blockaded with fugitives; and so most of the scores of thousands had nothing to do but fly right before the destruction that pursued them. Daylight had dawned, but the sun was blotted out by the dense pall of smoke, and hope too was well nigh obscured. Behind rolled the awful billows of that sea of fire whose extent they could only imagine, and here and there before them a flying brand had lighted a new fire that might ere long cut off their retreat. "To the lake!" was the instinctive cry of thousands, and soon the beach of that great but now almost useless reservoir was lined with the frantic multitudes and such effects as they could save. But the relentless demon pursued even here, showering upon them his rain of fire, and many preserved themselves from actual burning alive only by covering their bodies with blankets, frequently removed to be soaked in the water. Farther up the shore many sought refuge in the old burying-ground, hiding themselves in the vacant graves; and many wretched hearts, weighed down with the loss of every earthly possession and fearing that they had looked their last upon dear ones from whom the frenzy of the flight had parted them, earnestly wished for the peace of the new-made grave and the protection of the grassy mound which fire cannot penetrate and beneath which the trampling hoofs of flame are never heard.

Ere long Lincoln Park, the resort of gayety and fashion, was thronged with the fleeing multitude; and here some security was found, the walls of green keeping back the tide of fire, though falling brands flashed momentarily among the distracted groups and set fire to treasures painfully brought hither, after repeated removals, only to be consumed. Thousands and thousands more stopped not to trust themselves even here, but pushed on, miles to the northward, to the open prairie beyond the city; and there night overtook them, homeless, foodless, illy-clad, exhausted, almost broken hearted. That night of cold and rain, by the lake shore, among the tombs, in the dark woods, and upon the desolate waste, with neither fire nor food nor shelter, formed a fitting close of the horrors of that awful day.

If amid woes like these, strong men who had met death on the ocean and the battle-field, the young and healthful who still had life to hope for, the wealthy who still had an abundance left — if these should sink in despair, what were the woes of tender children, dragged from their beds to meet the flames, separated from their protectors, tortured by fears that their little minds could not comprehend; of delicate women — many, alas! in that supreme moment when other lives are wrapped up in their own; of the sick, the bed-ridden, the dying, hurried from their chambers into the wild street and borne helplessly hither and thither with the fever breath of the fire upon them; of the aged — the gray-haired fathers, the mothers bowed with years and cares, for whom life, even with the pleasantest surroundings, had lost every charm, and whose only wished-for boon was a quiet death-bed, surrounded by those for whose happiness they had spent their lives;— how can we picture the appalling aggregate of these bitter sorrows? Let us drop the curtain over the tear-compelling picture, thanking God that somehow men and women live through such tremendous scenes as we have faintly described, and that most of the flying thousands, escaped from the furnace and from the jaws of famine and destitution, still survive, and with recovered courage and more of thankfulness than they ever knew before, are joining hopefully to repair their ruined fortunes and rebuild our well-nigh ruined city.

But some, alas! found in the flames their fiery winding-sheet. Sleeping in isolated buildings or in lofty stories of great blocks, or foolishly risking their lives to save their gold, some were stifled by the smoke, or burned alive as they fled, or fell with falling floors into seething pits of flame. The number of these unhappy victims can never be known, but it is certainly less than the appalling magnitude of the devastation would render probable. About one hundred and ten bodies have thus far been found, some scarcely scorched, and some charred and blackened and roasted into horrible, unrecognizable fragments of humanity. As the ruins of great buildings are removed, other remains will probably be found, and many others were doubtless so completely consumed as to leave no trace of their existence. Not a few of the lost, it is to be feared, brought their fate upon themselves by yielding to the stupefying influences of drink. One man at least was sacrificed on the altar of Mammon, for he was last seen climbing into an upper window of his burning house to rescue his secreted treasure of money, and in company with his lucre he perished. That the reader and those whom he loves better than himself escaped from the grasp of this fiery death, is a cause for gratitude that ought to make all his material losses seem unworthy of a moment's regret. *H. R. Hobart.*

Part III.—After the Fire.

THE BURNT-OUT PEOPLE, AND WHAT WAS DONE FOR THEM.

EVEN as, during those hours of furious burning, Panic and Terror, twin sisters in the family of the Furies, reigned supreme throughout the stricken city, so, immediately after the Great Fire, Chaos and Despair, the brothers of Death, became the ruling powers of the desolated town. The flames which had consumed the stores, offices, shops, and homes of thousands, had died out; but the dread consequences of their ravages remained. All was confusion and horrible uncertainty. The streets, alleys, houses, and doorways of the unburned sections of the city, as well as the parks and the prairies on the outskirts, swarmed with sad, terrified multitudes. Where to go, or what to do, they knew not. Some who, more fortunate than the many, had friends residing in the saved parts of the town or in the suburbs, took refuge with them, and were hospitably welcomed; others sought shelter in sheds, barns, and churches; others, having saved nothing but a few dollars, hastened to the railway stations and left for other cities. But there was still the homeless, foodless, unsheltered, destitute multitude — men, women and children, at least an hundred thousand of them — who knew not whither to turn, or whence to expect food, help or comfort. The streets and the lake and river shores beyond the limits of the smoking ruins, were thronged with moving, mingling masses of anxious wanderers—some with vehicles laden with a few articles of rescued household goods, but many on foot, walking about with uncertain purpose. Here and there, exhausted and in despair, lay or sat on sidewalks, lumber piles, or door-steps, grim-visaged men, weeping women, and sleeping children, as homeless as, and much more haggard than, the Gypsies or the Arabs. And, as if the troubles and anxieties of the unfortunates from the loss of their homes and property by the conflagration were not enough, evil-minded and desperate men took advantage of the virtual state of anarchy existing, to plunder such helpless ones as chanced to take refuge in out-of-the-way places, in courts and alleys; and the city was filled with terrifying rumors of incendiarism and murder and the summary execution of guilty ones Night came, and Darkness reigned queen of the hours, for the gas supply had been cut off — and the fears and anxieties of the homeless wanderers were almost unendurable. The police force was disorganized, demoralized, and powerless. There was no Power to control the confused elements, to protect the weak against the strong, or to enforce law, order or justice. That first night after the fire — that fearful Monday night of the 9th of October in Chicago — was as complete a picture of social, moral, and municipal chaos as the wildest imagination can conceive. No water supply, no light, no police protection, no security anywhere — drunken men reeling recklessly about and uttering coarse blasphemy — thieves prowling around the temporary refuge of the unfortunates — alarms of fires and wild rumors of assaults and shootings — and, more terrible still, the general fear that the wind would change from the southwest to the north, northwest, or east, and by blowing the heat and cinders of the burning coal-yards and the smoking ruins in the direction of the still standing parts of the city, cause another great conflagration, and consume what remained of the afflicted town: — the reader can try to imagine the scene; and when, as he contemplates the terrible picture, a shiver of horror runs through his frame, he may in a measure appreciate the sensations which tens and hundreds of thousands of human beings experienced all through that dreadful night, and which many of them experienced for even a whole week of days and nights.

How to bring order out of this chaotic condition of affairs, was the problem of the hour. The Mayor had telegraphed to other cities for help, and issued proclamations for the regulation of the police and the relief of the destitute. The first proclamation was as follows:

PROCLAMATION.

WHEREAS, In the providence of God, to whose will we humbly submit, a terrible calamity has befallen our city, which demands of us our best efforts for the preservation of order and the relief of suffering;

Be it known, That the faith and credit of the city of Chicago are hereby pledged for the necessary expenses for the relief of the suffering.

Public order will be preserved. The police and special police now being appointed will be responsible for the maintenance of the peace and the protection of property.

All officers and men of the Fire Department and Health Department will act as special policemen without further notice.

The Mayor and Comptroller will give vouchers for all supplies furnished by the different relief committees.

The headquarters of the City Government will be at the Congregational Church, corner of West Washington and Ann Streets.

All persons are warned against any act tending to endanger property. Persons caught in any depredation will be immediately arrested.

With the help of God, order and peace and private property will be preserved.

The City Government and the committees of citizens pledge themselves to the community to protect them, and prepare the way for a restoration of public and private welfare.

It is believed the fire has spent its force, and all will soon be well. R. B. MASON, Mayor.

October 9, 1871, 3 p. m.

This document, distributed throughout the city, had an instantaneous effect in bringing the police and those of the citizens who were helpfully disposed to the support of the Mayor and his subordinates in authority. His call for help was also promptly and generously responded to by the officers and people of other towns and cities. Car-loads of cooked food arrived by every train, and many wagon-loads were sent in from the surrounding country. These were distributed among the needy. The hungry were fed, so that the more terrible fate of starvation did not follow the destruction of the people's homes. The citizens organized a system of patrols, which, co-operating with the police force, guarded what remained of the city from the torch of the incendiary, and protected the persons and property of individuals against thieves and robbers. But these means of protection and security, though effective, were not deemed sufficient. It was felt, both by the Mayor and the citizens, that in the midst of such an extraordinary emergency, extraordinary measures were required. Fortunately the headquarters of Lieutenant-General Philip H. Sheridan, of the U. S. Army, commanding the military Division of the Missouri, were established in Chicago. That distinguished officer and his official aids had been active and energetic, both during and after the conflagration, in efforts to save the city and restore order. By their valuable services they demonstrated their appreciation of the emergency, and drew to themselves the gratitude and the confidence of the municipal authorities and the people. On Wednesday, October 11th, the second day after the fire, a conference between the Mayor, the Police Commissioners, and the Lieutenant-General, resulted in an arrangement by which the latter was entrusted with the superintendence of the city's peace. The Mayor proclaimed this fact to the public as follows:

PROCLAMATION.

The preservation of the good order and peace of the city is hereby entrusted to Lieutenant-General P. H. Sheridan, U. S. Army.

The Police will act in conjunction with the Lieutenant-General in the preservation of the peace and quiet of the city, and the Superintendent of Police will consult with him to that end.

The intent hereof is to preserve the peace of the city without interfering with the functions of the City Government.

Given under my hand, this 11th day of October, 1871. R. B. MASON, Mayor.

The Lieutenant-General entered upon his charge on the following day, having already telegraphed orders for the transfer of companies of his troops from Omaha and other points to Chicago. These arrived on Thursday night, and, together with the police and the volunteer military companies that had reached the city from Springfield, Champaign, Bloomington, Rock Island, and Sterling, were placed on guard duty in various parts of the city, as also was a regiment of volunteer patrolmen that had been organized by General Frank T. Sherman, a citizen, who had been an officer of the Volunteer Army of the United States during the late war of the Rebellion. Thus was the peace and security of the city restored. A feeling of safety was inspired throughout the community. Lawlessness and disorder were promptly suppressed, and those guilty of crime or attempted violence were arrested and locked up. This system of military protection was continued for several days, when, all serious danger having passed, and the police efficiency of the city government having been re-established, the Lieutenant-General was relieved of his charge, his companies of regulars were sent away, and the volunteer patrolmen were dismissed from service.

It is amazing how soon and how completely the indescribable confusion and chaos consequent upon the great conflagration were systematized and adjusted into order and regularity. And yet this restoration of order and this submission to authority were but the outward aspect of the situation. All was still dread uncertainty — painful anxiety. Even those whose faces smiled and who spoke words of cheer and encouragement to their friends and neighbors, carried in their breasts heavy, anxious hearts. The merchants, who had lost their stores; the capitalists, whose buildings had been reduced to ashes; the bankers, whose treasure-filled vaults were covered with the *debris* of crumbled and fallen walls; the lawyers and physicians, whose offices had been swept completely out of existence; the publishers, editors, and printers, whose types and presses were destroyed; the manufacturers, whose machinery and tools had been transformed into molten masses of rubbish; the preachers, whose stately churches were now ghastly ruins; the thousands of clerks and mechanics, whose occupation was utterly gone; the hotel proprietors and their guests, who were now in a common condition of homelessness; the managers and artists of the theatres and opera houses, whose temples now lay flat with the earth; and the thousands of families, rich and poor, whose homes had been thus quickly devoured by the insatiate and unsparing fire-fiend; — all — alas, how many there were of them! — were in a common agony of suspense and despair; and the wonder is that, under such a strain of nervous excitement, mental anxiety, and physical exhaustion, continuing for days and nights, the entire population did not become a community of lunatics. Millionaires had become beggars; merchant princes and landed lords had become bankrupts; none knew how it was with them, or how it would be; *now* they were thankful if they could find bread to eat, water to drink, or where to lay their fevered heads. Men were like ships which had lost their anchors, — adrift in mid-ocean, without chart, compass, or destination. Painful uncertainty was reflected from every face, while utter despair was so plainly apparent in some countenances that one could read their sorrowing thoughts as on a printed page.

But as every storm is succeeded by a calm, and as every dark night is followed by the light of a new morning, so were the hopelessness and despair of those first few days immediately succeeding the Great Fire followed by rays of cheer and promise, dim and fitful at first, but gradually growing brighter and steadier in their effulgence, until the entire community became, as it were, illuminated with hope and encouragement. The discovery that the contents of the bank vaults and of many of the iron safes in business houses were uninjured, removed a heavy burden from many anxious minds; and the announcement that at least some of the great insurance companies that had Chicago risks would pay their full losses, and that probably the rest would pay a goodly percentage, also had a cheering effect. The repair of the City Water Works and the restoration of the water supply, after ten days' suspension, was another element of relief, as a few days subsequently was the restoration of the gas supply to the unburned portions of the afflicted divisions of the city. The prompt re-appearance of the daily newspapers, eloquent with cheering words and timely counsels, and filled with the blessed tidings that the whole country and the world at large had been moved, as if by magic, to a sympathetic response to Chicago's great disaster, and were contributing vast quantities of food and clothing, and even vaster amounts of money, for the relief of the destitute thousands, inspired the sad and stricken people with new courage and hopefulness; and this effect was hastened not a little by scores of sympathizing visitors and helpers from abroad, and by a flood of letters to citizens from friends, creditors, and capitalists, proffering not only words of sympathy but acts of generous assistance.

In the mean time, many who at first supposed that they had lost everything, found that they still had enough left for a new "start in life," and some were even so fortunate as to discover, after examination of bank vaults, safes, and insurance, that they had *much* left; these, however, were rare exceptions to the rule. A large number of small dealers, manufacturers, professional men, and others, had lost everything but their wits, courage, and energy, which, in most cases, were their original capital in business, and which, it is hoped, will again serve them to good purpose in their efforts at recuperation.

The re-opening of the banks of the city was one of the marked events of the emergency. In ten days after the fire, all the banking institutions, having found new locations, opened their doors for business, and instead of an exhaustive and panicky "run" upon them by depositors, general surprise was occasioned by the fact that few depositors wished to take their money out of the banks, while many offered funds for deposit. There was no excitement, no panic, no "run." This remarkable fact was especially unexpected as regards the savings banks, in which many of the poorer classes had placed their savings, which, it was anticipated, they would now be anxious to take out, both because of their actual necessities and for the reason that they were fearful of the ability of the banks to weather the sudden storm. This feature of the city's after-the-fire experience was most gratifying and stimulating. It was felt that the banks being safe, solvent, and able to resume their legitimate business, confidence would be effectually restored, and the trade and commerce of the city be speedily re-established. And this was the effect. The grain trade, the cattle trade, and the lumber trade, in their respective marts, were in full and successful progress within a fortnight after the fire. The dry goods, grocery, and other merchants, some of whom constructed temporary wooden buildings for their accommodation on the lake front or in the burnt district, and many others of whom secured new quarters in the unburned districts, ordered new stocks of goods, and in less than three weeks many of them resumed business. At the same time general preparations were making for rebuilding ruined houses and blocks. The scene at the ruins was gradually enlivened by throngs of busy workmen engaged in clearing away the *debris*, taking out and piling up bricks and building stones, and in laying the foundations and walls of new buildings. "Never say die!" was the motto of all — in acts as well as in words.

But — to return to the scenes of chaotic confusion immediately after the conflagration — how about the multitude of families who had lost their homes and were driven out to the parks, prairies, and temporary places of refuge in the streets, sheds, and houses beyond the limits of the fire? Who cared for them? and what became of them?

There were Good Samaritans abroad in those sad, distressful days. Agents and officers of the city government did what they could, and private individuals — humane and thoughtful ladies and gentlemen of our city and of other cities — volunteered their kindly efforts to relieve and care for the houseless and foodless thousands. Churches, school-houses, and other public and private buildings, were suddenly transformed into barracks and hospitals, and tents were pitched in various places. Into these the unfortunates were invited for shelter, and there their necessities of food and clothing were supplied as best they could be. Many citizens opened the doors of their residences to friends and strangers alike, and provided for their comfort. Not a few of the refugees had either gone or been transferred from the parks and prairies to the suburban villages and farm-houses a few miles distant, and there found hospitable welcome. Thus, gradually but surely, was the great multitude of the destitute and suffering provided for. It was an herculean work to gather them all in and render them even tolerably comfortable, for they were many in number, of all ages and conditions, and the majority of them, as the result of the terror and exhaustion of their desperate flight from the threatening flames, were at first as helpless almost as infants, and all were in despair and nearly heartbroken. How could it have been otherwise, when they had lost their sacred homes, with all their household treasures, and been driven forth pellmell to seek refuge they knew not where? How could it have been otherwise, when, with nothing to shelter them but the broad canopy of the sky, and nothing left to inspire them with hope or cheer but their faltering trust in that Providence which they felt, in their hours of despair, had completely deserted them and left them to a desperate fate? How could it have been otherwise than crushing and heartbreaking to those who, whether yesterday rich or poor, to-day absolutely had nothing left but their own weary frames and the smoke and dust-covered clothes on their backs? The spectacle of an hundred thousand human beings thus quickly driven, terror-stricken and destitute, to seek refuge from peril and death, and gathered in trembling and disconsolate groups in fields and along roadsides — men despairing, women agonizing, and little children crying for something to eat and to drink — is a new one in this country; and even in the older countries of earthquakes, plagues, or other terrible visitations, just such an one as this at Chicago after the Great Fire, with its attendant horrors, has probably never been witnessed.

But when the great work of gathering in and caring for these suffering people was once fairly begun, as it was only a few hours after the conflagration had burned itself out, it was not long before in the hearts of even these hope and courage were inspired; and even they, notwithstanding their terrible straits, discovered that, though they had lost much, all was not lost. They discovered — and it did their hearts good — that there is a truer brotherhood in the common family of mankind than they had ever before supposed — a brotherhood which only needs to be made to feel and to see that we are all poor, helpless, miserable creatures when the Great Father of us all withdraws His protection from us even for a moment, to impel it to the adoption of the Christian rule, that as we would be helped when in need, so must we help others when they need our help. They discovered that charity not only began at home, but came in from abroad — came to their relief, kept them from starvation, and helped to lift them up out of that "slough of despond" into which they had been plunged as if by the strong arm of the Lord.

After a few days of official and private effort for the relief of the homeless sufferers, the Mayor, perceiving the vast extent of the work to be done and the necessity that it should be done systematically, judiciously, and thoroughly, determined to turn over the entire care and responsibility of the city relief to the Chicago Relief and Aid Society — an incorporated organization of citizens, which had previously had charge of the dispensation of charitable aid and comfort to the worthy poor in the city. The officers and agents of this Society, being experienced in the work of caring for the needy, and being gentlemen and ladies of acknowledged benevolence, good judgment, and integrity, the Mayor acted wisely when he transferred this great and complicated business of practical relief to them. The Society at once entered upon the discharge of its sacred and arduous trust. It receipted for and took into custody the vast contributions of food, clothing, and money that poured in from all parts of the country, Canada, and Europe, and adopted a comprehensive system of distribution of aid to those needing it. At the same time the citizens of Cincinnati established and supported, and by their own agents conducted, a free soup-house for the benefit of the hungry, at which hundreds were daily fed; and it is the intention to continue the same through the winter. The Relief Society at first fed daily about 80,000 people, but the number soon diminished to about 60,000, many having secured remunerative employment, and others having taken advantage of the generous liberality of the railway companies, who, on application of the proper officers of the Society, granted free passes to all wishing to go to other parts of the country. The Society has also issued to several hundred heads of families sufficient quantities of lumber with which to build frame houses for themselves. The relief work is carried out with a degree of systematic regularity, care, and good judgment, that insures help for all worthy persons who are sufferers by the fire, and at the same time rejects the applications of imposters and of able-bodied persons who can, if they will, find employment and earn their own living. We are well assured that the contributed stores and funds — the results of the world's generosity — are being carefully and faithfully applied, and that the desires of the donors are being conscientiously carried into effect.

The spontaneous and general response of the people of various parts of our own country and of other countries, when the startling tidings of Chicago's great calamity were received by them, was one of the most remarkable and significant features of the event. Chicago was one of the nerve centres of the world's social and commercial system, and the blow that fell upon it thrilled and excited the whole of Christendom. The electric wires that flashed the startling news to the uttermost parts of the earth, brought back, as if in a return wave, great throbs of sympathy and sorrow, which told us in eloquent language that wherever civilized man dwelt, our overwhelming disaster was the subject of grief, and our people the objects of pity and benevolent regard. First and foremost of the towns and cities that responded with sympathetic words and tears and with generous offerings of help and relief were those which had been Chicago's most jealous rivals in Western commercial ambition — Milwaukee, St. Louis, and Cincinnati. Each of those cities was shocked as if by an earthquake by the news of Chicago's sudden and terrible calamity, and instantly hastened to her assistance. Milwaukee and St. Louis sent fire engines and car-loads of provisions by the same trains, reaching us in "the nick of time." Cincinnati sent provisions, clothing, and money, without stint or measure, and noble "angels of mercy" were sent with them to administer comfort and relief in our hour of anguish and despair. How suddenly every feeling of rivalry or unfriendliness between these cities vanished, and was followed by the sweet and gentle spirit of charity! How the bruised and heavy heart of stricken Chicago throbbed out its thankfulness and its deep gratitude to its humane neighbors! How quickly rivals in commerce became rivals in magnanimity; and how, in a feeling of common sorrow, enemies became friends, and bitterness was changed into loving kindness!

Nor was the "humanity of man" confined to those three cities. The small towns and the country people adjacent to Chicago were first heard from — they did what they could for us, for they were of us; and every town and city in the West and in the East, some of those in the South, a number of those in the New Dominion of Canada, even many of those in Great Britain, France, Germany, and Austria, and the city of Havana in Cuba, speedily and generously sent us welcomed sympathy in sweet words and needed help in substantial gifts. Municipal governments voted money — some a hundred thousand dollars, others less, but many very liberal sums — for the "Chicago relief fund." The cities of San Francisco, Memphis, Indianapolis, Louisville, Cleveland, Pittsburg, Buffalo, Rochester, Syracuse, Utica, Albany, New York, Philadelphia, Baltimore, Washington, Providence, Boston, Portland, Montreal, Hamilton, London, and others — and so many others that we have not room to give the entire list — offered to us handsful of money and food, and were eager to bring more if we should need more. Up to the last day of November, the cash contributions received by the Chicago Relief and Aid Society, amounted to about $3,000,000.

Smarting under the crushing blow of our affliction, we first groaned and wept with very pain; but when the sympathies and treasures of other cities and of the country and the world at large came pouring, like the oil of healing, in upon us, our tears of sorrow were changed to tears of gratitude and joy, and with reddened eyes looking heavenward from amid our ruined metropolis, we thanked God for the nobility of human nature. Our sorrow was a new one and a great one, but its burden was greatly alleviated and its pangs mitigated by the new revelation that it caused to break in upon our tearful vision — that grandest revelation of the humanity of man that has ever brightened the history of our race — a revelation at once so surprising and so glorious that it has filled us with a stronger faith that there is much that is divine in the nature of mankind. It has been a general supposition that man is naturally and essentially a selfish being — that, for the sake of self, he will sacrifice friends, principles, and honor, — and that genuine charity is a rare treasure that can be found only by digging down deep into the human soul. But the blow which struck down Chicago also struck that chord of humanity which vibrates with the sympathetic thrill of a common brotherhood — the chord which unites us all, and makes the great family of man a grand unit in impulse, sympathy and a sense of dependence. Men who had labored for, and garnered and watched with a miserly vigilance, the accumulations of a life-time, suddenly tore loose from the cold, clutching grip of avarice, and emptied their treasured thousands into the hands of Bounty, for Chicago's relief in her hour of sore distress. Opulent and grasping corporations, to which general sentiment had denied the possession of souls, astonished the world by their munificence in gifts and favors to the afflicted city. Competing and rival towns and cities no sooner heard of our overwhelming disaster than they poured out their wealth for our relief. England, forgetting the old-time prejudices against American ways, institutions and pretensions, fairly turned her "horn of plenty" upside down over the lap of ruined and suffering Chicago. Germany, flushed with her freshly-earned triumphs in the land of the vanquished Gaul, for the moment lost sight of her occasion for rejoicing in her sympathy with the grievous calamity that had come upon this youngest of the great cities of the Republic across the sea. Austria, debt-burdened and tyrant-tied, was moved to make offerings for our help; and even France, paralyzed and impoverished after her stunning defeat at the hand of the Teuton, drew forth a ready hand from her almost empty pocket, and sent to us what she could hardly spare. The close-fisted Yankees of New England, the slow-plodding capitalists of Canada, the lavish spendthrifts of the Pacific Coast, and the "peculiar people" of Utah — all contributed with liberal hands. And what was least expected of all, cities in the lately rebellious South, which owed Chicago no friendship, were among the first and most generous in their benevolence in a time when "friends in need were friends indeed." Surely it is true, as Shakespeare — human nature's faithful interpreter — makes Ulysses say, that

"One touch of nature makes the whole world kin."

And we verily believe that the world has been made better by Chicago's fiery ordeal. The hearts of men had long been growing hard and cold, and needed just such a shock to soften and warm them to generous impulses. Whatever brings soberness to the wild and reckless spirit; whatever tames the rash and dashing steeds of worldly ambition; whatever draws out our thoughts and loves from within ourselves and away from the follies of the world, and opens up and enlarges our sympathies and regard for our brother man, — has the effect to make better men and women of us. Heavy and grievous as this blow has been to us, it has not been without its benefits, both to ourselves as the suffering victims and to the rest of mankind as our sympathizers. It has made us less presuming, less proud, less boastful, and taught us humility and the uncertainty of all earthly things; and it has broken the iron shell of the world's avarice, stimulated and developed its humane impulses, and enriched it by the discovery of treasures of benevolence and "sweet charity" before hidden and unknown. Fire destroys, but it also purifies. Affliction and sorrow are hard to bear, but they also develop the real heroism of the human soul. "Man proposes, but God disposes," is the grand lesson of the history of the ages.

Andrew Shuman.

AMONG THE RUINS.

GRAND as was the tumult of the fire, with its motion, its omnipotent energy, its unsurpassed colorings, and its human agony, it scarcely excelled in this direction the contrasts that were developed in the ruins. There, was no life, color, motion, or strength. As that seemed the embodiment of vast, resistless force, this appeared the incarnation of pitiable weakness. The one swelled, roared, surged, towered; the other was silent, sombre, dull, inanimate.

The four or five days which immediately succeeded the *Dies Iræ* — the Black Monday of Chicago's life — were the period in which the ruins presented their most effective character. During that time, stupefaction prevailed among the people; and men neither attempted to measure nor repair the calamity. Walls lay as they fell; the *debris* were untouched; yawning walls, broken columns, shattered chimneys, and slender, smoke-stained arches extended everywhere in a wilderness of undisturbed profusion.

It was at this time that one could best appreciate the character of the catastrophe. Standing upon Madison Street bridge, one had a *coup d'œil* beneath which desolation reigned supreme. The air was curtained with an apathetic smoke, through which grotesque and distorted remnants were revealed, and whose prevailing hues were the pallor, the ashiness, the presence of all the tints characteristic of death. Even the strong sunlight gave no brightness to the smoking area, but, on the contrary, seemed to intensify its ashen complexion, and to make more conspicuous its leaden characteristics. Gray, the white of cheeks emaciated with disease, funereal black, and an uncleanly, sickly red; — these were the tints that made up the picture, and which were all in harmony with its sadness and its depression.

Not one look, not a score of examinations, would enable one to comprehend what extended before him. The sadness, the extent, the desolation, grew with each inspection. Each study brought out new features, that never lightened but which always intensified those already discovered. All the characteristics of chaos and destruction seemed present, and none failed to present themselves as a reward for patient and extended study.

One remarkable feature was that found in the complete obliteration of all recognizable characteristics of places and localities. There seemed a resolute purpose on the part of the spirit of destruction to sweep from existence even the suggestions of the proud piles of marble. Whole blocks were hurled to the ground so evenly that street, alley, or this or that land-mark had disappeared as completely as did Herculaneum under the ashes and lava of Vesuvius "Somewhere yonder was my building," was a frequent remark; and it was only when the work of clearing away in recognizable localities had been commenced, that many a citizen was able to establish points of observation whereby the location of his tumbled walls could be discovered.

In squares which had been occupied by wooden structures, the work of destruction was as complete as if the whole had been caught up and borne away. Here, absolute annihilation was the rule. Block after block would reveal no evidences of there having existed civilization, save the excavations of the cellars and a thin layer of ashes. Nothing unconsumed remained. The very air seemed to have been on fire; and, under the enormous heat, wood was reduced to an impalpable dust, and all metals shrank away in liquid rivulets and disappeared.

A stranger, ignorant of the occurrence of the fire, might have travelled over acres without scarcely meeting a single thing to even suggest that the areas through which he was passing had ever been inhabited; in many instances, he would hardly suspect even that there had been a fire, so complete was the work of annihilation. So consuming was the fire that, in many cases, it not only obliterated everything constructed by man, but even licked clean the usual traces of its progress.

The great contrasting effects of the conflagration did not occur between the fire and the ruins — although there was, as has been noticed, the difference between the potent, resistless energy of the one, and the quiescent weakness of the other — but between the city as it was on Sunday, and the same as it appeared twenty-four hours later. Strong as was the contrast between the vividness of the fire, with its crimson banners blazing athwart the whole sky, and the ashen desolation, the ineffable sadness and quietude of the ruins, there was a more noticeable contrast between the white and shapely marble acres of one day, and the dull, prostrate, sullen remnants of the day which followed. This was a contrast whose effects and characteristics men had leisure to observe; but that which the fire afforded them was so hurried in birth, so awful in its progress, and so stupefying and prostrating in its existence, that no man had leisure or presence of mind or inclination to make it a study.

But of the nature of the stately piles which reared themselves so superbly skyward on Sunday, and of the character of the disordered and smoking mass which represented them on Monday, men have had ample time for the study. To the citizen, the fire is no more than an incident, a terrific lightning flash, which had scarcely time to impress itself on the memory. The desolation, then, does not recall the sublime occurrence of a world aflame, of stars foundered in a crimson ocean, of a vast population, frenzied, despairing, flying; but brings back only our beautiful city as it was, and invites an almost hopeless interrogation of the future.

There was one single feature of the ruins that almost approached the character of an amelioration. This one feature came into existence during the moonlight nights that soon after succeeded the calamity. Even then there was nothing of a nature to lessen the severity of the affliction; but there was something to soften it, somewhat as a wreath of flowers takes something from the horror which is born of the pallor and the rigid immobility that possess the face of the dead.

Nature seemed desirous of affording such relief as lay in her power; and thus it happened that, during the day, the genial sun, his rays inspired with warmth and kindness, flooded the ruins in golden profusion, while at night the pitying moon silvered over the harsher features of the desolation, and gave them a tinging of softness and quiet repose that at least rendered their examination less a labor of sad depression. At such times, a journey through the ruins, in place of giving birth to sinister suggestions, awoke the artistic nature of the observer, so that what before seemed a monotonous and afflicting calamity, became a softened and pleasing study. One could forget the dollars burned, the families homeless, the material consequences of the fire, and entertain himself with the artistic beauties of the scene.

True it is that in these inspections there was nothing exhilarating. It was somewhat of the nature of a stroll through the well-trimmed walks, handsome monuments, and green surroundings of a cemetery. One admired its beauty, while there weighed upon him the conviction that he was in the midst of a dread influence that repressed everything that approached hilarity or even exaltation.

And thus men and women wandered through the burnt district by moonlight, fully appreciative of the spirit of the calamitous influence, and soberly and silently pervaded with the artistic beauty of the picture.

Nothing could be more novel and finer than these moonlight effects. Everywhere were contrasts shorn of harshness, and pervaded with harmony and interests. Banks of deep shadows lay behind walls, and met beyond, and united everywhere with masses of silvery light. The moon seemed to touch all with a gentle, pitying hand. Infinite softness and gentleness pervaded the silvery pall, as if nature understood that it rested upon something whose snfferings entitled it to a forbearing consideration.

One of the most noticeable effects developed at night was connected with the burning of the small coal piles in the basements or yards of what had once been dwellings. For many days after the fire, these continued burning, but not with a hasty, devouring flame. From the rounded surface of each of these small piles, there rose spires of flame a few inches in height and of a pale blue color. These agitated by the breeze, bent and swayed, and seemed like buds of violet waving in the wind.

Everywhere these fairy-like flower-buds of flame met the view, and added to the scene a wierd and indescribable beauty. In the chastened *demi-jour* character of the light, the black surfaces of these flame flower beds came distinctly into view, and afforded an exquisite contrast with the lurid, lanceolate spires which waved tremulously above them, and which, although adding no light to the landscape, came into brilliant distinctness, and merged harmoniously with the brighter light of the moon.

Another noticeable moonlight feature was the thousands of blackened trees that were met at almost every step. All of these had their branches pointing rigidly to the northeast, the direction in which went the gale that bore the torrents of fire over the city. Black, rigid, lifeless, bent, and pointing towards the quarter where went the storm, they seem murdered victims whose last effort before dissolution was to arrange themselves so as to fix a thousand motionless and accusing arms to point out the hiding place of their destroyer.

Already have the Ruins of Chicago become almost a thing of remembrance. Brick walls have risen like an exhalation from among their disorder, and whence the smoke struggled up sullenly and where the moon flung a pitying veil, there now are thronged the temporary structures which are the overture to Chicago's architectural resurrection. The grand, far-reaching ruins are narrowed into scars, and, in a little time, under the healthful operations of the circulation of Chicago blood, even these will be obliterated. Gone already is the first hideousness of the destruction; and scarcely before the world shall have recovered from the moral shock of the event, the Ruins of Chicago will exist only in remembrance, or upon the canvas of the artist.

F. B. Wilkie.

RECONSTRUCTION.

FROM that windy night when the first prophetic flame shot into the clouds and leaned like a crimson Pisa to the northeast, till the last building fell and the destroyer had crept sullenly away into coal piles and garbage heaps, there was a helpless acquiescence on the part of spectators that was pitiful. But when the raging fiend had died of plethora, the old energy again came forth. Rigidity returned to the weakened spine and vigor to the flaccid hand, and the eye of enterprise was lighted up once more with its undying flame. When the fire was baffled, citizens who had cowered and fled before it in awe arose bravely and said, " We can conquer everything else."

On every one of the hundred squares that had been laid in ashes on the South Side, men straightway attacked the smoking embers, extinguishing the lingering flames in order to build anew. Pieces of iron, writhing in a thousand fantastic forms, and scarcely revealing under their strange disguises the original gas and water pipes, safes, scales, chandeliers, stoves, mantels and columns they had been, were pulled out while still warm, and carried away for foundry purposes. Ashes and broken bricks were carted to the lake, and dumped, to make more land for an already opulent railroad corporation. Walls were pulled down, and an army of men were employed to completely clear away the *debris* and clean and square with a trowel such bricks as could be made available for rebuilding.

The first merchants who returned to the burnt district were, of course, the newsboys, peripatetic of habit and insinuating of demeanor. After the newspaper nomads, came an **apple-woman** on Tuesday morning, who, with an air of mingled audacity and timidity, stationed her hand-cart at the corner of State and Randolph Streets, half a mile within the ashen circle. She was the pioneer of all the trade of the future. On Tuesday morning the last house burnt, away at the north. By Tuesday afternoon, a load of new lumber had crept into the South Division. On Wednesday morning, that lumber was thrown into the form of a box to cover a merchant's wares. This was the inauguration of Slabtown. Thenceforward there were innumerable cartings; heaps of charred rubbish were briskly exchanged for heaps of fresh pine; carpenters multiplied like locusts; the air assumed a resinous odor, and the clatter of hammers echoed as if the ruins were being knocked down to relic-hunters by an enraged auctioneer.

By far the most grotesque phase of the calamity is the manner in which the vast business of the city, suddenly driven into the street, instantly accommodated itself to new locations and conditions. When the crimson canopy of Monday night merged into the dawn of Tuesday morning, it was found that, besides personal property, some thousands of loads of merchandise had been saved — stowed away in tunnels, buried in back alleys, piled up all along the lake shore, strewn in front yards through the Avenues, run out of the city in box cars, and even, in some instances, freighted upon the decks of schooners off the harbor. And, far more than this, five thousand merchants had saved their Good Name — that imperishable entity, that "incorporeal hereditament," which resists burglars and all the assaults of the elements, and carries an invisible treasury for him who wears its badge. Two hundred thousand people in the city, and ten times that number out of the city, were in immediate need of goods and compelled to buy.

It was at this juncture that the terrible descent of the barbarians upon our aristocratic thoroughfares began. Down Wabash and Michigan Avenues, hitherto sacred to the "first families," rushed the Visigoths of trade in a wild, irresistible horde, with speculation in their eyes. West Washington Street — prim and stately West Washington — was the next victim; then followed West Lake, Randolph, Madison, Monroe. Block after block was swallowed up by the invaders — Trade walked into the houses with a yard-stick for its stiletto, and domestic life took up its pack and retreated.

Many a man who has done a business of half a million a year, has invaded his own front parlor on the Avenue; has whisked the piano, the gorgeous sofas, the medallion carpet and the clock of *ormolu* into the capacious upper stories, and has sent his family to keep them company; while show-cases have been arrayed through drawing and dining rooms, and clerks now serve customers with hats, furs, shoes, or jewelry, where they formerly spooned water ices at an evening party. The burnt district looks as if Cheyenne had waltzed across the alkaline prairies and bestridden our poor disreputable river; but the city for a mile west and south of the fire district looks like Vanity Fair. The carelessness, even recklessness, with which Commerce has dropped down into dwelling-houses hap-hazard, is grotesque and whimsical to the last degree. Three or four kinds of business, moreover, are crowded under every roof. A shoe store is in the basement, with long strings of gaiters and slippers hanging where the hat-rack was, a bench for customers improvised from an inverted box where the sideboard stood; fertile boxes of shoes are in the kitchen and coal-hole. And over the front windows five yards of outstretched cotton cloth bears the simple legend "SHOOES." Up stairs is a button factory, with pendulous and fascinating strings of buttons festooned across the aristocratic windows. The bed-rooms higher up are lawyers', doctors', insurers' offices; and into the dormer windows of the roof shoot a large quiver full of telegraphic wires. The next building is a stylish structure with a bow front; a bank president occupied it in September, and is perchance still an exile in some of the upper stories — but the bow window in the parlor, scene of what countless sly flirtations and pleasant family siestas, is now garnished with ladies' stockings hung up in graduated array; while a brown balmoral, swinging, a silent sentinel, at the door, and the variety of feminine toggery here and there displayed, complete the story of Mammon's invasion. Further on is a pretty cream-colored cottage, the obvious creation of a pair who were at once lovers and artists. It is set a little distance from the walk; it has the angles and wings that are so charming and picturesque; a veranda runs cosily around it, and along and about it climbs a vine — a cool and delightful summer trellis. Here, too, the barbarians have effected an entrance and broken up the nest. Barrels of molasses and vinegar and flour lie impudently and lazily in the yard. A greasy-looking man goes into the door with a kerosene can, and a boy sidles out giving his undivided attention to candy. In the bay-window is a symmetrical cob-house, constructed of bars of soap; and brooms, mops and codfish are disclosed through the leafless trellis.

A little further down the block a bevy of school-girls issue chattering from a ladies' fancy store; laces, collars, cuffs, velvet ribbon, and all the more delicate furniture of the female form, are displayed in the window and revealed through the door ajar. A month ago this was a blacksmith shop, and the sparks flew in a fountain from the anvil and the hammer clattered upon a horse's shoe. Scrubbing-brush and whitewash-brush have completely disguised the *parvenu*.

Down State Street to Twentieth — and here is the largest dry goods store in the city or the West: Field, Leiter & Co.'s. Here are hundreds of clerks and thousands of patrons a day, busy along the spacious aisles and the vast vistas of ribbons and laces and cloaks and dress-goods. This tells no story of a fire. The ladies jostle each other as impatiently as of old, and the boys run merrily to the incessant cry of "Cash." Yet, Madam, this immense bazaar was six weeks ago the horse-barn of the South Side Railroad! After the fire, the hay was pitched out, the oats and harness and equine gear were hustled into another building, both floors were garnished, and the beams were painted or whitewashed for their new service. Here, where ready-made dresses hang, then hung sets of double-harness; yonder, where a richly-robed body leans languidly across the counter and fingers point-laces, a manger stood and offered hospitality to a disconsolate horse. A strange metamorphosis! — yet it is but an extreme illustration of the sudden changes the city has undergone.

All up and down Wabash and Michigan Avenues on the South Side, and Monroe, Madison, Washington, Randolph, and Lake Streets on the West Side, the fronts of the houses have been suddenly adapted to new uses; extensions have shot out from the basement to the sidewalk, resinous with the smell of new pine; and signs have appeared in all sorts of uncanny places — spiked to the handsome front door that servants in livery used to swing open upon its bronze hinges, sticking awkwardly from the oriole window where the canaries used to sing, and even sprouting strange arborescent growths from the bit of greensward between the sidewalk and the street, multicolored, huge, and cruciform, on duty like so many bucolic warnings to "look out for the locomotive." Ever since the fire, Chicago has been the Mecca of sign-painters; and every man commanding a brush and paint-pot was sure of constant employment at high wages, whether he could spell or not. Pine boards have become exhausted, and broad bands of white cotton have been introduced instead;

and by such wrinkled insignia did some of the wealthiest of the National Banks first indicate their retreat.

The churches that are spared have been curiously appropriated — several of them by the Relief Societies, others by institutions that are of the earth earthy. Here is one overrun and utterly deluged by Uncle Sam's mail — given up in all its parts to the exigencies of the city postal service. One is divided up for offices: a lawyer offers to defend your title; an insurance man volunteers to save you from the next fire; and in the recess that used to hold the choir, a dentist holds the heads and examines the mouths of his victims. Another church is turned into a watch factory; and still another is possessed by an express company — and over the official desks in the vestry-room vaults in a painted bow is the suggestive legend, "Come unto me, all ye that are heavy laden."

As already intimated, the work of rebuilding began the instant the fire withdrew. Indeed, for weeks before the flames were extinguished, while fierce volcanoes smoked and glowed in every block, and the vast heaps of anthracite threw forth angry pink and purple tongues, like the geysers of the Yellowstone, thousands of men were finding the old dimensions of the cellars and building up the stone foundations anew.

The burnt district in the South Division—the square mile bounded by the lake, river, and Harrison Street—is too valuable per front foot to furnish hospitality to sheds, barracks and wooden warehouses like those that have found room elsewhere among the ashes. The real estate market, as far as there is a market, shows no great diminution below the prices asked and paid before the fire, and taxes over all these hundred blocks are still so heavy as to render prompt rebuilding imperative. So it happens that at the date of writing more than half the cellars again present the form of rectangular excavations swept and garnished for the builder's force. On each side of every square, eager teams drag up the inclines into the street great loads of brick, stone, iron, and ashes, and the foundation walls rise in their places again to the cheery cry of "Mort!" as, wooed by the strains of Amphion's lute, rose the conscious walls of Thebes. In the cellars of warehouses, where great masses of iron were kept, in stove stores, scale stores, and wholesale stores of hoop-iron, men, armed with drills, crowbars, huge sledge-hammers and blasting powder, are toiling to disengage the mass. Even the iron was as straw in the furnace-blast of that awful morning,—stoves, and sheet and pig iron, all melted miserably and ran helplessly down, roaring with rage, to the ground, and there it cooled in all fantastic attitudes and shapes. Here is a hillock of solid iron, as large as an omnibus; there is a platform as large as Table Rock—it once was moulded into kitchen stoves; yonder are upright masses, some of them rearing like a centaur, and others writhing like the group of the Laocoon; further down the ruins is a building where the lower stratum of the flowing metal has cooled first, and subsequent cascades of iron have dashed over it and trickled through it like so much molasses; and beneath, the drippings hang in iron crystal stalactites, from an inch to six feet long, like the lime drippings of a cave! As these are the most marvellous of the relics, so they are the most difficult to dispose of, and the owners of the lots are now quarrying the ponderous masses with huge levers, blasting powder, and all the arts of engineering.

The walls of more than three hundred of the better class of brick and stone buildings are already rising in the South Division — rising even in mid-winter, when masons are driven to cover in every other city north of 35°. Who thinks of using a trowel all through the winter months in New York, Boston, St. Louis, or even Cincinnati? Yet three thousand masons and bricklayers and mortar makers and carriers are regularly employed in Chicago all the week through, as we write. Many builders have halted at the top of the cellar wall to wait for March, but hundreds of others are pushing vigorously upwards in spite of every obstacle presented by an extreme climate. It is December, but an artificial summer is created to keep the work from freezing up ; a bonfire is blazing before the mortar bed where the compound is prepared as the housewife prepares her dough; and other and smaller fires blaze briskly all around within the rising wall—a fire on every mortar-board, which keeps the mortar plastic and the blood of the brick-layer uncongealed. Thus is the smitten city rising again at New Year's—rising, as she fell, by fire.

The number of brick and stone buildings in process of erection on the first day of December, on each street in the South Division, was as follows:

River street	8	Polk street	1
South Water street	12	Michigan avenue	3
Lake street	10	Wabash avenue	17
Randolph street	6	State street	24
Washington street	6	Dearborn street	6
Madison street	29	Clark street	16
Monroe street	26	La Salle street	4
Adams street	2	Fifth avenue	6
Quincy street	1	Franklin street	9
Jackson street	1	Market street	3
Van Buren street	1	Miscellaneous	21
Harrison street			
		Total	212

It is probable that a thousand stone and brick buildings will be in process of erection by May.

After the fire, the Board of Public Works issued one-year permits for wooden buildings, which virtually abrogated the ordinance forbidding them within prescribed limits. In four weeks thereafter, the North Side was covered with wooden buildings so thickly that it was difficult to see across the blocks, and a row of similar structures in the South Division soon stretched along the hitherto unoccupied Park, on the east side of Michigan Avenue, a mile and a half, from the river's mouth to Twelfth Street. Two stories only were allowed, but some became very capacious warehouses, adapted to the largest demands of a wholesale traffic.

The gravest peril of the city now lies in the prolonged existence and ceaseless multiplication of these combustible piles of lumber. Fire limits were prescribed by a timid Common Council in the hour of its dissolution, but the ordinance is openly violated in every part of the city with perfect impunity. The first man has yet to be arrested or annoyed for furnishing food for the next great conflagration. It would seem that Chicago could scarcely afford an *encore* of the performance of October 8–9; but a repetition of that tragedy is just as certain to follow the persistence in our clapboard and shingle madness, as is any given effect to succeed an adequate cause.

There is scarcely any city on the continent so exposed to prolonged and terrible winds as Chicago. Our constant imminent menace is that autumnal southwest hurricane which sweeps up from the wide prairie to the lake, eager to seize upon a spark and nurse it into a conflagration. Let a block get well on fire towards the Stock Yards in some densely settled locality, in the face of such a gale, and all the apparatus of the fire department must prove futile. Nothing but acres of solid brick or stone buildings that are virtually fire-proof can stop it.

W. A. Croffut.

Part IV.—THE LOSSES.

REAL AND PERSONAL PROPERTY.

THE extent of the devastation was so great, and the wreck so widespread, that a description of the area burned over and of the pecuniary losses entailed, can scarcely convey an idea of its magnitude, more than a statement of the distance of a fixed star enables us to bridge the gulf between it and the earth. And though we may apply the measuring rod to the scene of the carnage, and reduce into dollars and cents the value of the property destroyed, there are many and comprehensive losses not susceptible of a pecuniary classification. There are tens of thousands of material things that elude the attempt to assign them monetary worth; much less can we fix a value on the sum total of human happiness lost and human life destroyed by the dread visitation.

Grave difficulties exist, too, in the way of ascertaining the extent of even the more tangible losses, though several weeks have now elapsed since the event. The destruction was so complete that it not only obliterated the property itself, but swept out of existence the records of its value and the evidences of proprietorship. And in the last-named fact we have another most perplexing element introduced into the previously complicated problem, which if not rightly treated would involve us in the most inextricable confusion. The loss of title to real or personal property does not necessarily involve the loss of that property to the community. What is lost to one in this way, may be gained by another.

In this article we shall try to answer the questions, What was burned up? and What was the amount of loss to the community as a whole? leaving untouched the equalization of the numerous differences arising between individuals as a result of the catastrophe. Hence we make no allowance for the loss of evidences of title or indebtedness, because those documents simply indicate in whose hands the property in question shall rest. Yet it would be unfair to include bank notes under this head, for, though really nothing but certificates, they were actually accepted and used as money, and it will be some time before the place of those bills will be supplied by others: though not in existence, they are still recognized as liabilities by the banks that issued them.

For the same reason, we disregard the item of insurance on property burned. It was very consoling to the policy holder to find that he was insured in companies that would pay a hundred cents on the dollar. But this only settled the question as to how widely the loss should be distributed, and who should bear it. In the case of many of those who were the most wealthy before the fire, the question was even less important than this. Their property was insured, but they were also large stockholders in the insurance companies; so that if the insurance were good, it would simply amount to an offset of one loss against another.

Neither would it be fair to swell the total with allowances for expenses incurred in caring for property during the fire, or the increased cost of replacing it, owing to the higher price of labor and material; because these incurred expenditures inure to the benefit of the persons receiving the money, which is not, therefore, lost to the com munity. In regard to losses on the rental of property, an allowance ought probably to be made, but these are largely counterbalanced on the general account, by the enhanced rentals secured on property not touched by the fire. The most important allowance in this direction will be that due to the interruption to the trade and commerce of the city — the temporary suspension of the productive energies of the people.

The questions to be answered are, then, How much property was destroyed ? and What was the value of the property consumed by the flames ?

In the West Division, where the fire originated, the number of acres burned over was 194, including sixteen acres which were laid bare by the fire of the previous evening. This district contained about 500 buildings, inhabited by 2,250 persons. These buildings were generally of the poorer class, and comprised a great many boarding-houses, saloons, and minor hotels, with a few factories. They were not of much value, but were closely packed together. This district contained also several lumber and coal yards and planing mills, one grain elevator, with the union depot of the Pittsburg and Fort Wayne, and the St. Louis Railroads. This depot was much the least valuable of all those destroyed.

The burned area in the South Division comprised about 460 acres. With the exception of the Lind Block, on the river bank, between Randolph and Lake Streets, it included all north of an irregular line running diagonally from the intersection of Polk Street with the river, to the corner of Congress Street and Michigan Avenue. This district, though comparatively small in extent, was by far the most valuable in the city ; it was the very heart and head of Chicago as a commercial centre. It contained the great majority of all those structures which were at once costly in themselves, and filled with the wealth of merchandise that made the city the great emporium of the Northwest. All the wholesale stores of any considerable magnitude, all the daily and weekly newspaper offices, all the principal banks, the leading hotels, many extensive factories (principally of clothing, boots and shoes, and jewelry), all the offices of insurance men, lawyers, produce brokers, etc., the Custom House, Court House, Chamber of Commerce, all the principal public halls and places of amusement, many coal yards, the monster Central Railroad Depot, with its numerous buildings for the transaction of business of the Illinois Central, Michigan Central, and Chicago, Burlington and Quincy Railroads, the Central Elevator A, the Union Depot of the Michigan Southern (Lake Shore), and Rock Island and Pacific Railroads, many public storehouses, a large number of fine residences on the Avenues ; in short, the great bulk of the wealth of the city was located in this district. The 3,650 buildings destroyed in the South Division included 1,600 stores, twenty-eight hotels, and sixty manufacturing establishments, and were the homes of about 21,800 people.

In the North Division, the flames swept not less than 1,470 acres, destroying 13,300 buildings, the homes of 74,450 people, and leaving but about 500 buildings unharmed. These structures included more than 600 stores and 100 manufacturing establishments. Most of the latter were situated in the southwest part of this division, in a few blocks lying east of Kinzie Street bridge; but there were also many on the north bank, towards the lake shore, including McCormick's Reaper factory, a sugar refinery, box mills, etc. The lake shore, from Chicago Avenue north, was lined with breweries. The river banks were piled high with lumber and coal, three grain elevators stood near the fork of the river, and near them the Galena depot, its freight buildings further to the east Many hotels and private storehouses for produce and other property also existed in this neighborhood, and the wholesale meat markets on Kinzie Street were a busy centre of trade. North Clark, Wells, and North and Chicago Avenues, were principally occupied by retail stores. The region south of the Water Works and east of Clark Street was at one time the most aristocratic part of the city. It contained a great number of fine buildings, occupied principally by the earliest settlers or their families. This district included many churches, the Rush Medical College, the Historical Society building, with its treasures, etc. Outside of this section the buildings in the North Division had been, till recently, of the poorer class; but the establishment of Lincoln Park, and the closing of the old cemetery, had caused a radical change in this respect within the five years preceding the fire. A large number of very fine residences had been erected in the neighborhood of the Park, and a great improvement was apparent in the architecture of the whole North Division, except one or two small sections, which seemed to have been tacitly given up to poverty and its accompaniments.

The total area burned over in the city, including streets, was 2,124 acres, or nearly three and one-third square miles. This area contained about 73 miles of streets, and 17,450 buildings, the homes of 98,500 people. The following were some of the most important structures burned :

Among Public Buildings were, the Court House, consisting of a central portion erected in 1853 and enlarged in 1857, and two wings, each 80 by 130 feet, and three stories high besides the basement; a handsome stone structure, costing altogether about $1,100,000. The Custom House and Post Office, erected in 1858-9, by the General Government, cost $650,000. The Chamber of Commerce, erected in 1864-5 at a cost of $225,000, besides a building on the south used for offices, the total cost being $284,000. The principal building was constructed of Athens marble, and covered an area of 91 by 180 feet; the basement and first floor were occupied by banks, insurance offices, and prominent produce dealers. Above these was the Exchange Hall, 88 by 143 feet, with a 44-foot ceiling, in which the 1,250 members of the Board of Trade used to transact business. With these we may note the city property other than the Court House; the Armory, Huron-st. and Larrabee-st. police stations, five fire-engine houses, several hook and ladder buildings, and eight bridges ($200,000). The public schools burned were the Jones, Kinzie, Franklin, Ogden, Pearson-st., Elm-st., LaSalle-st., and North Branch schools, with several adjunct buildings.

The railroad property destroyed included the Central Depot, at the foot of Lake Street, with several other buildings, occupied as offices for the Illinois Central Land Department, the Michigan Central and Chicago, Burlington & Quincy general offices and freight depots, besides which the dockage of the Illinois Central Railroad Company was considerably damaged; the depot of the Rock Island and Michigan Southern Railroads, the Galena depot, and some wooden structures belonging to the West Side Union depot.

The Grain Elevators burned were, the Central A, National, Galena, Hiram Wheeler's, and the Munger and Armour. These contained 1,642,000 bushels of grain. Considerable quantities of grain were also burned up in several smaller warehouses (private) in the North Division.

The halls, theatres, etc., included the Opera House, built in 1864, with Beethoven Hall, in the State Street front; Farwell Hall, the home of the Young Men's Christian Association; Metropolitan Hall Block, occupied by the Young Men's Library Association; the Museum Block; McVicker's Theatre, rebuilt in 1871, and reopened only a short time before the fire; Dearborn Street Theatre; Hooley & Aiken's Opera House, on the former site of Bryan Hall; Academy of Design;

Olympic Theatre; German Theatre; and Turner Hall.

The Hotels burned included the Sherman, Tremont, Bigelow, Palmer, Briggs, Adams, Metropolitan, St. James, Revere, Nevada, Massasoit, Matteson, City, Clifton, Hatch, Anderson's, Burke's, Central, Eagle, European, Everett, Garden City, Girard, Hess, Orient, Schall's, Hotel Garni, Howard, Hutchinson's, New York, Washington, and Wright's.

THE PALMER HOUSE.

The daily newspaper buildings were those occupied by the *Tribune; Times; Journal; Republican; Staats Zeitung,* and *Post; Mail,* and *Union,* and *Volks Zeitung.* The offices of THE LAKESIDE MONTHLY were in the *Tribune* Building.

The list of church property burned is an extensive one; it comprises the following: Baptist — North, Second, German and Swedish, North Star, and Lincoln Park Mission. Congregational — New England and Lincoln Park. Episcopal — Ascension, St. Ansgarius, St. James, and Trinity. Jewish — North Side, Sinai, Kehilath Benai Sholom, and Hospital. Methodist Episcopal — First (business block), Grace, Van Buren Street, Clybourne Avenue, First Scandinavian, Bethel (colored), Quinn's (colored), and $85,000 worth of Garret Biblical Institute property. Scandinavian Lutheran — First Norwegian, and Swedish. Presbyterian — First, and Mission, Fourth, Bremer Street Mission, Erie Street Mission, and Clybourne Avenue Mission. Roman Catholic — Holy Name, St. Mary's, Immaculate Conception, St. Michael's, St. Joseph's, St. Louis', St. Paul's, Convents of Sisters of Mercy and Good Shepherd, St. Joseph's Orphan Asylum, Christian Brothers' College, Alexian Hospital, and Bishop's Palace. Swedenborgian — Temple, and North Mission. Unitarian — Unity. Illinois Street Mission, and Mariners' Bethel.

Among business blocks the following were the most prominent, each being worth $50.000 or over: Arcade, on Clark, near Madison; "Booksellers Row," on State, near Madison; Bowen's, on Randolph, near Michigan Avenue; Bryan, corner of La Salle and Monroe; Burch's, on Lake, near Wabash Avenue; City National Bank; Cobb's, corner of Lake and Michigan Avenue; Commercial Building, corner of La Salle and Lake; Commercial Insurance Company's, on Washington, near La Salle; Depository, on Randolph, near La Salle; Dickey's, corner of Dearborn and Lake; Drake & Farwell, corner of Wabash Avenue and

DRAKE AND FARWELL BLOCK.

Washington; Ewing, on North Clark, near Kinzie; Exchange Bank, corner Lake and Clark; First National Bank, corner State and Washington; Fullerton, corner Washington and Dearborn; Field, Leiter & Co. (Palmer's), corner State and Washington; Honore (two), on Dearborn, near Monroe; Illinois State Savings, on La Salle, near Washington; Keep's, on Clark, near Madison; Kent's, on Monroe, near La Salle; Link's, corner Lake and La Salle;

Lill's Brewery; Lloyd's, corner Randolph and Wells; Lombard, corner Monroe and Custom House Place; McCormick's, corner Lake and Michigan Avenue; McCormick's, corner Randolph and Dearborn; McCormick's Reaper Factory, near Rush Street bridge; Magie's, corner La Salle and Randolph; Major, corner Madison and La Salle; Marine Bank, corner Lake and La Salle; Masonic, on Dearborn, near Washington; Mechanics', on Washington, near La Salle; Mercantile, on La Salle, near Washington; Merchants' Insurance Company, corner Washington and La Salle; Monroe, corner Clark and Monroe; Morrison, on Clark, near Monroe; Newberry, corner Wells and Kinzie; Newhouse, on South Water, near Fifth Avenue; Oriental, on La Salle, near Washington; Otis, corner Madison and La Salle; Pope's (two), Madison, near Clark; Portland, corner Dearborn and Washington; Purple's, corner Clark and Ontario; Raymond's, corner State and Madison; Republic Life Insurance Company, corner La Salle and Arcade Court: Reynolds, corner Dearborn and Madison; Rice's, on Dearborn, near Randolph; Scammon, corner Randolph and Michigan Avenue; Shephard's, on Dearborn, near Monroe; Smith & Nixon's, corner Washington and Clark; Speed's, on Dearborn, near Madison; Steele's, corner La Salle and South Water; Sands' Brewery; Turner's, corner State and Kinzie; Tyler's, on La Salle, near South Water; Uhlich's, on Clark, near Kinzie; Walker's, on Dearborn, near Couch Place; Wicker, corner State and South Water.

The following valuation of losses was prepared by the writer for Colbert & Chamberlin's "History of Chicago and the Great Conflagration":

BUILDINGS.

Eighty business blocks, enumerated,	$ 8,515,000
Railroad depots, warehouses, and Board of Trade,	2,700,000
Hotels,	3,100,000
Theatres, etc.,	865,000
Daily newspapers (offices and buildings),	888,000
One hundred other business buildings,	1,008,420
Other taxable buildings,	28,880,000

Churches and contents,	2,989,000
Public Schools and contents,	249,780
Other public buildings, not taxed,	2,121,800
Other public property (streets, etc.),	1,763,000
Total,	$53,000,000

PRODUCE, ETC.

Flour, 15,000 barrels,	$ 97,500
Grain	1,245,000
Provisions (4,400,000 lbs),	340,000
Lumber,	1,040,000
Coal,	600,000
Other produce,	1,940,000
Total produce,	$5,262,500

BUSINESS — WHOLESALE AND RETAIL.

Dry goods,	$ 13,500,000
Drugs,	1,000,000
Boots, shoes, leather, etc.,	5,175,000
Hardware, iron, and other metals	4,510,000
Groceries and teas,	4,120,000
Wholesale clothing,	3,650,000
Jewelry, etc.,	1,300,000
Musical Instruments, etc.,	900,000
Books on sale,	1,145,000
Millinery,	1,610,000
Hats, caps, and furs,	1,060,000
Wholesale paper stock,	700,000
Shipping and dredges,	800,000
Manufactures (stock, machinery, and product),	13,255,000
Other stocks, and business furniture,	25,975,000
Total Business loss,	$78,700,000

PERSONAL EFFECTS.

Household property,	$ 41,000,000
Manuscript work (records, etc.),	10,000,000
Libraries, public and private	2,010,000
Money lost (Custom House $2,130,000),	5,700,000
Total personal effects	$58,710,000

GENERAL SUMMARY.

Improvements (buildings, etc.),	$ 53,000,000
Produce, etc.,	5,262,500
Manufactures,	13,255,000
Other business property,	65,445,000
Personal effects,	58,710,000
Miscellaneous,	378,000
Grand total,	$196,000,000

In the first table the contents of churches and schools and of newspaper offices are included in the footing of $53,000,000. Placing these where they belong, we shall have the following distribution of loss:

On Buildings, etc.,	$ 52,000,000
On Business Property (besides bldgs.),	85,000,000
On Personal Effects,	59,000,000
Total burned,	$196,000,000

On this there was a salvage of about

$4,000,000 in foundations, and bricks available for re-building, making the actual loss $192,000,000.

The assessed value of the land in the city, just previous to the fire, was $176,931,900, which was about sixty per cent. of the actual cash value. Hence the real value of the land within the city limits was $294,836,000. On this we estimate an average depreciation of about thirty per cent. since the fire, though much of this can be but temporary. This gives a loss of $88,000,000 on the selling value of real estate in consequence of the fire.

Even yet the total of loss is not complete. We must allow for the interruption of business and manufacturing operations. This would average about six weeks, or one-eighth part of the whole year. We estimate that the fire diminished the receipts of the city to the extent of $50,000,000 worth of goods, which interrupted business to the extent of $125,000,000 worth of trading, at wholesale and retail. The very moderate estimate of eight per cent. profit would give a further loss of $10,000,000, and we shall then have the following as the exhibit:

On Property burned up,	$192,000,000
On depreciation of Real Estate	88,000,000
On interruption to business,	10,000,000
Grand total,	$290,000,000

We estimate the value of property in the city the day before the fire, real and personal, taxed and untaxed, at $620,000,000. The loss by the fire was, therefore, nearly forty-seven per cent. of the whole of the property owned in Chicago. *Elias Colbert.*

COMMERCIAL AND PUBLIC INSTITUTIONS

DURING the terrible Monday, to the question, "In what company are you insured?" the uniform answer was, "It makes no difference now; insurance is worthless." That was the almost universal feeling. Gradually the sober second thought came, and men began to hope. The distrust of insurance companies was not a conviction,—it was rather a part of the general smoke. As soon as men began to reason, the rays of hope began to shine. It was seen at once that all underwriters had some assets, and every one must pay in full or be put into the hands of a receiver. Sufferers then began to cast about, to look up their papers if not destroyed, and if they were to ask if they could not be restored. And so by degrees this second stage of uncertainty gave way to definite knowledge of what to expect.

A bird's-eye view of the situation showed that insurance was good, as a rule, in proportion as it was a good ways from home. The foreign risks of Chicago amounted to only $6,000,000. Those were all "placed" originally in a few very heavy English companies. Then, too, it is the custom across the water to distribute risks among neighboring companies. But even without this prudent system of distribution, all those policies would have been paid, dollar for dollar. It was equally obvious at a glance that home insurance was next to worthless; that every company doing any considerable amount of home business had vastly larger losses than capital. One home company, the Great Western, was an exception, owing to its youth; and another, the American, escaped the general crash because it had no local risks. Still another, the Republic, after being in a peculiar "dead and alive" condition for several weeks, finally announced that its losses would be paid in full — an assessment upon its stockholders having been made to supply the deficiency between its assets and losses by the fire. With these exceptions, all home companies went down in the common wreck.

The following table shows the aggregate loss of the companies by States, the number of companies in each State, and the number suspended:

STATE.	NO. OF SO.	AGGREGATE CAPITAL.	TOTAL GROSS ASSETS.	TOTAL LOSSES	NO. SUS- PENDED.
New York	193	$30,161,232	$54,675,350	$21,637,500	20
Ohio	50	5,896,753	7,988,076	4,818,657	5
Massachusetts	34	5,051,800	13,380,703	4,483,500	3
Pennsylvania	34	5,025,800	13,582,044	2,082,000	1
Missouri	20	2,783,254	3,088,034	575,000	1
Illinois	18	4,314,951	5,789,917	33,878,000	14
Maryland	11	2,837,651	4,133,003	397,165	4
Connecticut	11	6,700,000	13,829,884	9,325,000	1
Kentucky	9	2,000,000	2,224,543	6,800	7
Rhode Island	7	1,900,000	3,116,836	2,072,500	6
California	3	3,753,600	5,730,630	2,950,000	
Michigan	3	400,000	620,463	175,000	
Maine	2	550,000	900,161	30,000	
Wisconsin	1	314,175	374,883	290,000	
Minnesota		120,000	280,593	100,000	
New Hampshire		100,000	134,586		
Total of U. S.	335	$74,939,21	$135,420,426	$82,821,122	57
Foreign	6		10,459,095	5,813,000	
Grand Total	341		$145,879,521	$88,634,122	

The failure of the Prince Albert of London, a few years ago, and of the Home of Hartford, shook public confidence in distant companies. The general feeling was, in Chicago at least, that a home company was safer because its affairs were open to full inspection. The adoption of our present system of State supervision, by the General Assembly of 1868–69, strengthened the confidence in all fire risks.

It is always easy to find fault, and after any great disaster point out blunders. Much unjust censure has been heaped upon Chicago insurance companies. No one is to blame for not anticipating such a sweeping conflagration, and our companies were quite as sound as the average of the three hundred and thirty-five in the country. They all have manifold greater liabilities than capital. If they did not, there would be no profit in the business. The underwriting system is based upon the supposition that it is safe to have about thirty dollars of risks to one dollar of capital. The losses of United States companies by this one fire exceed their aggregate capital by nearly $8,000,000; and eighty-seven of them were not affected at all, and only fifty-seven have suspended. The grand mistake made was in taking such vast risks in one city. A great conflagration is always possible; and had the Chicago fire been one-tenth its actual proportions, it would have been no less fatal to our local companies. Home policies are the least desirable of any, because the flames which destroy the property insured may destroy the assets of the insurer. Hartford is the insurance capital of the country; and it is noticeable that while the entire losses of Connecticut were only $9,325,000, those of New York were $21,637,500, and those of Illinois foot up $33,878,000. The policy of distribution seems to have been adopted by the older companies before this latest and plainest lesson was given.

The especial insurance lesson of the Great Fire is this: Distribute risks. If one city can burn up, any city can. In no one place should a company assume liabilities beyond its power to pay, in case of a general conflagration. State legislation should guard against this grand mistake of our insurance system as at present conducted.

The solicitude in regard to the insurance companies was absolute indifference in comparison with the anxiety about the banks. There are twenty-seven of these institutions in Chicago, counting only those belonging to the Clearing House Association. In what condition their vaults would be found, no one could tell; and in most cases the valuables were all stored in those repositories. It was known that the vaults of the Court House and Custom House were not fire proof, and the wildest rumors were rife about this and that bank. For several days the heat was so intense that no examination was possible. That was a terrible suspense. All the buildings and goods destroyed were of less value than the currency, notes, bonds, bills of exchange, and other papers, in the vaults of those twenty-seven banks. Squads of soldiers guarded them day and night. In the meanwhile the bankers met to discuss the situation. A committee was appointed to draw up a programme. The President of one National Bank stood alone in simply saying, "Gentlemen, there is only one way: go ahead as usual, paying dollar for dollar. If we cannot do that, we must wind up." The others were either silent, or said, " Even if our vaults are all right, we cannot pay in full at once." The committee agreed upon recommending that they should resume by paying an instalment of twenty-five per cent. When that report was made, the president of another bank—a man whose wealth was reckoned by millions—protested that the figure was too high, and insisted upon its reduction to ten per cent. The final agreement was upon fifteen per cent. The Comptroller of the Currency at Washington, Hon. H. R. Hurlburd, at once telegraphed to the National Banks to await his arrival before resuming. He arrived on the Saturday following the fire. By that time the vaults had been opened, and all but one bank was unscathed. The only exception was the Merchants Savings Loan and Trust Company; and it was only the account-books of that bank which perished. On Sunday the Comptroller met the bankers, and the whole subject was discussed. That official insisted that the true policy was to resume in full. In this opinion he was inflexible. His *ultimatum* was that if any National Bank failed to resume in full as early as three o'clock of the following Tuesday, he should put a receiver in charge of its affairs. The consequence was that every bank announced that it would resume business as usual, Tuesday, October 17th.

The effect of bank resumption was more than magical. Not a single banking house in all Chicago, small or great, failed. The solvency of our banks was the first positive assurance the country had that Chicago would rise from her ruins. Talk is cheap, whether of the tongue or the types. What the press said needed the substantial indorsement of the banks. Board of Trade circulars, mercantile encyclicals, and all that sort of thing, were useful; but the leverage of finance was indispensable to raise the fallen prestige of desolated Chicago, and convince the world that the City of Ashes had vitality enough to recover itself.

There were two things accomplished by the bank policy: First, the capital and capacity already here were induced to remain; no business deserted the city; it was only the flies upon the coach wheel which flew off; stalwart men took heart, and nerved themselves for the work of reconstruction. Second, outside capital and enterprise were drawn hither at once; and the men who came here did not come as wreckers to pick up the waifs of the storm, but, hopeful for Chicago's future, they came to cast in their fortunes with its regeneration, by aiding to repair the ravages of the fire.

In looking back at this terrible ordeal, the close observer sees that it was a severe test of the soundness of our National Bank system. In 1857, the failure of one bank in Cincinnati brought our whole monetary institutions to the brink of ruin; and a host of them actually passed over the cataract and were lost. There was a fatal defect in the system. It was an arch without a key-stone. One of the loose bricks gone, and the whole pile fell. Now we have a system so compact that it can stand any conceivable shock. The fire test of last October was severer than any "hard times." We need have no fears hereafter that our financial system will come crashing down upon us. Whatever else may befall, we may dismiss all apprehension of such a disaster. The real secret of the solvency of our banks is that our monetary interests are so indissolubly interlinked, that a common necessity was bound to hold them up.

Of the public buildings destroyed, one of the most important was the Water Works, which was one of the first points on the North Side reached by the fire. The wind was in exactly the right direction to cover the roof of that structure with cinders. The massive walls were fire-proof, but the roof was of "composition," tar, gravel, and paper. The direct damage sustained was $200,000; but the indirect was vast beyond computation. It cut off our water supply, and thus rendered our fire department useless. Some buildings in the heart of business would otherwise have been saved. The terrible anxiety of the fire week was largely due, to the fact that the usual means for stopping a conflagration were powerless. Not making the building which sheltered the Water Works' engines absolutely fire-proof, was a monstrous blunder.

The city lost no less than one hundred and twenty and three-fourths miles of sidewalk, to replace which would cost at least $1,000,000. It is to be hoped that a fire-proof material will be used in the future. The Nicolson pavement suffered but slight damage.

The total loss to our Public School department amounts to $502,600, of which $297,800 represents the value of reference books, libraries, etc., on which there was no insurance. Of the buildings destroyed, two, the Kinzie and Jones, were very old and dilapidated, and would soon have been torn down to give place to better structures. The following is the list:

SCHOOLS.	LOCATION.	VALUE.
Jones,	Cor. Harrison and Clark,	$ 9,000
Kinzie,	Cor. Ohio and La Salle,	16,800
Franklin,	Cor. Division and Sedgwick,	73,000
Ogden,	Pearson near Dearborn,	35,000
Pearson,	Cor. Pearson and Market.	12,250
Elm,	Cor. Elm and North State,	12,750
La Salle,	Cor. La Salle and North Ave.,	23,000
N. Branch,	Vedder, near Halsted	23,000
Value of buildings.		$204,800
Value of libraries, etc.,		297,800
Total,		$502,600

The Fire Engine and Police Station losses figure up $196,350. There were seven bridges burnt. Instead of rebuilding them, there should be tunnels excavated in some cases if not in all. In a thronged city, a swing-bridge is an insufferable nuisance, and should give place as soon as possible to a tunnel.

By far the greatest loss of the city and county was the Court House. That massive piece of botch-work, with its two wings, was a sham; and could its contents only have been saved, the loss of the building itself would not have been deplored. It will it is thought take about $2,000,000 to erect such a structure as the needs of the county and city require. The General Assembly, at its Fire Session, convened by the Governor immediately after the conflagration, assumed the debt contracted by Chicago in the construction of the Illinois and Michigan Canal, amounting to nearly three millions of dollars—it being stipulated that the money should go to rebuild the Court House and other public structures. To this proposition there was no hostility whatever in the Legislature or the press of the State.

As even the Court House vaults were a sham, the incalculably valuable records of the city and county were destroyed. The loss of those archives was a disaster which no human intellect can so much as apprehend, not to say comprehend. There were the official records of all the real estate transfers in Cook County; of all the mortgages on real and personal property; the archives of all the courts, including the papers on unfinished probate business; the official minutes of the proceedings and final actions of all county and city legislation. In fine, everything of a public documentary character which was in the keeping of the city or the county, went to feed the ravenous flames.

The greatest immediate evil is the delay in settling probate business, and the utter impossibility of proving many valid claims in favor of heirs. The irretrievable loss to widows and orphans will be millions. In ordinary judicial proceedings, old cases will, if renewed at all, have to be conducted largely upon equity principles and in accordance with chancery practice. It is safe to say that fully one-half the cases on the several dockets at the time of the fire will never be renewed. Litigation will gradually extricate itself from the present dilemma; and it is quite likely that the average result, except in probate business, will be as equitable as it would have been had the records been preserved. At least there is no general solicitude on that score.

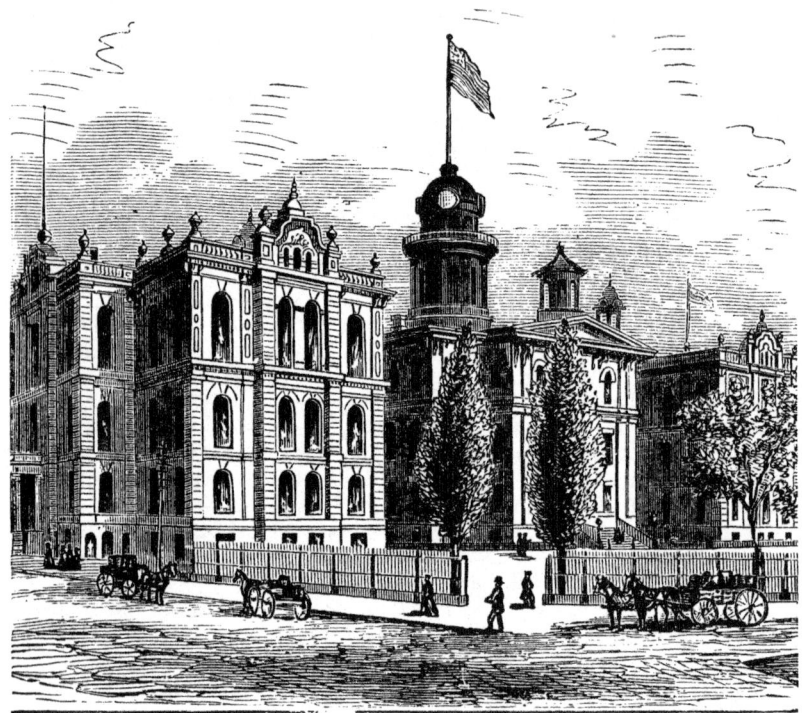

THE COURT HOUSE.

The loss of the official records of deeds and mortgages was appalling. The great value of a city is its real estate. The ground of the burnt district is to-day worth hardly less than all the property destroyed. To unsettle titles would be terrible. Indeed, the city would not rise again had that actually occurred. But, fortunately, there are three complete unofficial abstracts of records which were preserved. To look up titles in the records as kept by the county would have been a very tedious job. To economise time, private enterprise had made out abstracts of all those official records, from which any one could in a short time find out the validity of any given title. So reliable are those abstracts that it was very rare for any one to go beyond them in the investigation of a real estate title. Practically, therefore, we have left a complete chain of evidence to prove every land title in the county which was unclouded before the fire. These books are the salvation of Chicago. Had they been destroyed, titles could not be substantiated without the delay of a chancery trial, and in the meanwhile building operations would have been suspended and commerce would have sped away to other localities. As it is, it only remains to purchase — or, if the owners value them too highly, "condemn" under the State's sovereign right of eminent domain,— all those records; through a competent commission compare them and make out a certified copy, and then legalize, or make official, said certified copy. In that way the loss can be retrieved and the peril of insecure real estate titles be averted.

The Water Works was one of the first public buildings reached by the fire, the Custom House the last. The former was farthest from the origin of the fire, the latter nearest. All the United States officials in Chicago had offices in that building, except the Pension Agent, the Internal Revenue Assessor, the Register in Bankruptcy, and the Steamboat Inspector. The third floor was wholly given up to the judiciary. All the official papers of both the Circuit and District Courts, and of the U. S. District Attorney, and of the Marshal, were destroyed. Nothing was taken from that floor, and everything was a total wreck. Fortunately, Judges Drummond and Blodgett have both been in the habit of making out abstracts of all the cases tried before them, which they forwarded to Washington. These will be of great service in straightening out federal court business. The official papers in the office of Judge Hibbard, the Register in Bankruptcy, were a very serious loss. Congress will probably pass a measure for bringing order of the chaos of the federal judiciary business at Chicago.

The second floor of this building was mainly devoted to impost business. The Collector of the Port, Hon. Jas. E. McLean, had general charge of the whole building, and besides the tariff affairs was custodian of the federal funds at Chicago. At the time of the fire he had in his keeping $400,000 in coin and $1,800,000 in currency. There were vaults on the second floor which were supposed to be absolutely fire-proof. In them all these moneys were stored. They also contained all the books and accounts of the office, besides private papers and memoranda of the employes and attaches of the establishment, the actual value of which will depend largely upon the honesty of the various debtors.

When the *debris* was cleared away, nothing remained but charred ruins. The coin was found to be fused, and had to be forwarded to the Philadelphia mint for re-coinage. The Collector of Internal Revenue had his office on the same floor. The actual loss from the destruction of his papers will be slight, as nearly all of importance had been duplicated and the duplicates sent to Washington. The same is true of the Assessor's papers. An act of Congress will be necessary to relieve both collectors of balances standing against them on the books at Washington, it being the practice of the Treasury Department to charge the collection of all taxes, internal and impost, to the Collectors. The passage of such an act will hardly meet any opposition, as the honesty and efficiency of both collection offices are undisputed.

The number of vessel arrivals at the port of Chicago annually exceed those of New York, Philadelphia, Baltimore, New Orleans, San Francisco, Mobile, and Savannah combined. The amount of bills of sale, ship mortgages, and general evidences of vessel property, which were recorded upon the books of this Custom House, were consequently immense. Their destruction will entail upon the owners a vast deal of trouble, although the duplicates forwarded to Washington will be of incalculable use in straightening out these tangles. There was, however, the period of three months just previous to the fire, the transactions of which had not been reported.

The first floor and the basement of the Custom House were wholly given up to the postal service. As there is always a corps of workmen in that department, day and night, and mail teams in stables near by, if not on the spot, the letters — of which there were probably no less than 150,000 in the building — were all taken out and carted to a place of safety. It is due to the postal service to add that although the Postmaster, Hon. F. A. Eastman, was himself a victim of the fire, as well as one hundred of the three hundred men in his employ, he and they made the public interest supreme, and in an incredibly short space of time had the machinery of the mails in good running order, making up and distributing letters with almost the usual promptness. It is a remarkable fact that in a vast number of cases friends at a distance received letters from Chicago before they did the telegram of the same date. Had it not been for the Great Fire, the completeness of our postal machinery and the efficiency of this branch of the service would not have been appreciated by the public. The letter-carrier system was eminently useful in facilitating business. On the old system of box delivery, postal business would have been hopelessly confused.

We have said that the State will virtually be at the expense of rebuilding the Court House. The United States will of course erect another Custom House. The old structure was altogether too small to meet the demands of federal business at this centre. The old site must be enlarged, and a building put up that shall be commensurate with the importance of the city. Every federal office should be under its roof. The expense will be a very small item, as compared with the means at command. It is expected that Congress will early pass an appropriation for the purchase of additional ground and the erection of a suitable building. The old one really had hardly room enough, all told, for the Post Office alone, or for the Custom House proper. For mail distribution, Chicago is second only to New York; and its growing importance as a port of entry may be inferred from the fact that the receipts of coin duty during last September were three hundred per cent. greater than they were during the corresponding period of 1870. There are two reasons for this — the establishment of a line of steamers running in connection with ocean steamers at Montreal, by which imports come through without the vexatious delay attending shipments by way of New York; and the passage of the direct importation act of July 14, 1870. The fire has not lessened our imports. On the contrary, the receipts of customs since the great calamity have been larger than ever.

At present the High School Buildings, located in the West Division, are made to take the place of the Court House, so far as possible. The federal offices are all located in the South Division, as near as possible to the centre of the city. The Custom House proper is at Congress Hall where it will probably remain until the erection of the new Custom House. The Wabash Avenue Methodist Episcopal Church, on the southern edge of the burnt district, has been fitted up for the Post Office. It will doubtless be three or four years before it will return to its old locality.

Chicago has had enough of huge tinder boxes. There is such a thing as absolutely fire-proof building structures, and such without doubt every one of our new public buildings will be. Then they will stand the shock of conflagration, let the flames rage never so fiercely, and hold fast their sacred trusts against the most desperate burglary of fire.

Hardly had the rills and rivers of charity began to flood our city, when landsharks put in an appearance, offering to buy real estate at "fire prices." Dealers also advertised to sell at "fire prices." The first class went away without investing, and the offers of the latter class were mere pretence. After careful investigation, we are satisfied that in the aggregate there was very little if any depreciation in the value 'of real estate, at least in the market price. The unclouded faith of all in the early reconstruction of the burnt district accounts for this fact.

While the aggregate value of real estate has not been affected by the fire, some changes have already been effected, and others may be expected. Particular localities which had been rendered specially valuable by some fortuitous accident have lost their advantage. Others, cursed by evil surroundings, have gained, making a "stand off." The most notable change of this kind is in the value of real estate near the river. Until last summer the river was so foul that it "poisoned" the property within smelling distance. Changing the current of the stream cleaned it, and rendered the banks habitable. But they were skirted with a class of buildings which repulsed mercantile houses. The fire, supplementing the change in the current of the river, paved the way for the wholesale business to push farther west than before, taking possession of a tract hitherto given up to fourth rate business. On the South Side, this will be the marked real estate peculiarity of the fire, viewed from the present standpoint.

To the superficial observer, it would seem that the value of the North Division real estate must have been depreciated. The improvements which made some of those streets the pride and beauty of our city have been swept away; but with the lake and Lincoln Park, it has its chief attractions left. It is secluded from the heart of business, yet not far off. It has now lost forever the old rookeries and riff-raff population near the river which were formerly such serious drawbacks upon the North Division. Then, too, those who had elegant grounds before the fire were interested in keeping down the value of real estate so as to escape heavy taxation. A man whose homestead occupied a whole block was necessarily a "bear" in the market. Now that part of the city will be built up as becomes residence property within a few minutes' walk of the heart of the city, and the "bears" will all turn "bulls." This change will be inevitable. These are the only changes in the value of Chicago real estate which have developed themselves.

Frank Gilbert.

RELIGIOUS AND EDUCATIONAL INSTITUTIONS.

THE fire was impartial in its destructiveness. Breweries and grain-elevators, saloons and banks, insurance offices and churches, all disappeared before it. Greenbacks passed beyond redemption, "fire-proof" safes melted, stones were shattered. The cold and passionless page is a poor medium to give any adequate conception of its power.

But some things proved indestructible. Even the wooden streets, so called, were more than equal to their purpose. The imaginations of persons at a distance pictured them as canals of flame, into which the terrified inhabitants leaped from the falling buildings; but art in their composition seems to have imitated nature, which makes her most substantial structures out of a happy combination of frail materials. The gravel and tar and wood together bade defiance to the heat. Had the sidewalks been made of the same material, and the houses, the sirocco which preceded the fire would have been soon forgotten.

Another imperishable thing was the soul of the city; not the absurdly vaunted energy of the people, but that combination of material and yet invisible forces which make Chicago a necessity. In the councils of eternity, the rivers, lakes, and prairies, when they assumed their proportions and relations, determined here the site of a large city. Chicago is where the water and land-carriages meet; in the heart of a country teeming with abundant products of air, earth, and soil, where streams of wealth must converge and again distribute themselves. It is a predestination that so long as that section of country called the Northwest has life, here must be its heart. There must be here a great concourse of human beings; and so long as the morals and habits of men and women are as now, this city will have its hovels and temples, its roughs and saints, and all the varieties which poverty and luxury and ignorance and both unbalanced and harmonious culture can produce. Vanity has claimed that it was due to the remarkable and almost preternatural sagacity and enterprise of a few men that Chicago grew so rapidly and awakened the astonishment of the world. "Scratch a Russian, and you find a Cossack." Unstrip the cockney Chicagoan, and you find an average white man (with few exceptions) parallelled by the great mass of human beings who pride themselves rather on their circumstances than on their merit. Chicago was originally a wet prairie, skirted on one side by dunes and gravel by the lake shore. There is certainly nothing in the atmosphere, pure though it be, from the lake and prairie, that should make its inhabitants superior to their neighbors. We do not hear that the few thousands who were driven away by the fire have started anywhere any new Chicagos. The thousands who have come in are fully equal to those who ran away. It may be seriously doubted whether, if all the three hundred thousand, not excepting its wonderful banking men, should betake themselves to Dogtown or Brush Four Corners, they would there reproduce the Garden City. They would soon scatter or starve. But if ten thousand young men and women could be selected by chance, out of the Caucasian or even the Mongolian race, and placed alone on the blackened bones of this Chicago, where the streets now project upward from the ground, like a huge skeleton, along the tri-river whose sluggish current still obeys the will of its late masters and flows inward rather than outward,—it would not be many days before the streams of grain and timber and coal and iron uniting there, on this heaven-made convergence of highways, would stimulate these strangers to seize their opportunity and exact the ordinary toll, put forth the required labor, and rise into wealth and power. Snow is found on the top of the mountain, flowers at its base, pearls in the oysters, and whales in the ocean; and cities, where alone so long as the world retains its present configuration they can be, and while the world abounds in men they must be, in the natural centres of industry and trade. To destroy a Babylon, the very people of the nation must perish. Art simply assists nature, and acts obediently to her laws.

In accordance with this theory, already buildings are arising on the burnt district by the thousand and by the mile, and it is to be hoped that, profiting by experience, there will be a better distribution and classification of the various kinds of industry than before. Painful as was the disaster, producing a shock both physical and mental that will prove fatal to many individuals, and beautiful as Chicago was, it is probable that five years hence the city will be, both as a place of residence and business, stronger and more pleasant than it would have been had the fire not occurred. And it is to be hoped that the public opinion of the city will exhibit in a larger degree the modesty that accompanies merit, and will waste no energy in boasting and no passion in useless sensitiveness to external criticism.

There is a large class of people in Chicago who are far more anxious about its intellectual and moral prospects than about its population or material resources. Great masses of humanity are not necessarily of much value to themselves or to the world. Babylon was not Athens; Constantinople is not Berlin. The cockneyism which leads an insignificant cipher of humanity to estimate his own value according to the long row of figures which the census of the state or nation employs where he lives, and in which he counts only one, is contemptible though common. A true man is of as much worth in a country village as in London, in Rhode Island as in New York, in Switzerland as in China. There have been cities which dying have left no sign, and whose influence when living was only that of dead weight. There have been country hamlets, single families, nay, individual men, worth more than a city full of trash. Intellectual and moral vitality, at least in the opinion of some, is of chief value. Chicago ought to be to the great Northwest what Boston is to New England — a centre and fountain of intellectual and moral power. In its short history, this city has had a fair proportion of men and women who have believed this doctrine and shown their faith by their works. Many of their enterprises have been arrested and destroyed by the fire.

The great rapidity with which the population here has been gathered, has rendered it impossible to provide means for the mind and heart commensurate with the demand, or equal to older cities of the same size. The public schools, admirable in their plan and actual character, yet left about a third of the children and youth without the means of public instruction. An inconsiderable proportion of the young men could withstand the temptations of the city and devote themselves to liberal study. Intemperance and vice destroyed thousands annually. The graduates of the high school were few compared with those of the same age sent to houses of correction and the state prison. No city should boast of its schools so long as a single child is deprived of their privileges for want of ample public provision. Five large public school houses were destroyed. As dwellings arise — no matter what may be the expense — school houses should be built at once, adequate to accommodate all the children. Let them, if need be, be less costly, and let the experiment be tried, if necessary, of having two schools accommodated in the same room at different hours of the day; but let no children be doomed to ignorance for want of free tuition. The various private schools that perished will undoubtedly be speedily re-established, as the motives that created them abide, and will easily find means of organization.

The museums, galleries of art, and libraries, must start again from the bottom. They had really produced but little effect on the public mind. Churches and mission schools abounded in the burnt district, though not in so large numbers as in the older cities. The great London fire two hundred years ago, though spreading over less than a fourth as large a space, and destroying a smaller number of dwelling-houses, yet consumed about three times as many church edifices as the Chicago fire.

It would be uncharitable to undervalue what the advocates of education, sobriety and religion have done and are doing in Chicago. This would betray a cynicism based on ignorance or prejudice. The deficiencies result from the rapidity of its growth. In the rank crop which springs up in a single season, there is always a predominance of weeds. Careful and persevering culture alone matures the most valuable growths. Magnificent wholesale palaces, with their stone and iron fronts, spring out of the percentage of profits which the streams of wealth that roll through the city leave behind. They are not extraordinary monuments of the sagacity or courage of their builders, any more than the tall corn of our prairies is an indication of extraordinary science and skill in our farmers. Why should not our capitalists build six or eight story stores and hotels of rock and iron? They are able, and obtain their reward in kind. But to found schools and museums and libraries and churches, and to use them according to the ideal of such institutions, implies patient thought and intellectual and moral culture, not necessarily engendered by a scramble for wealth or an ostentatious display of it. The Pilgrims built their meeting-house with their first dwellings. Chicago, if it has their spirit, while stores, hotels, breweries and saloons again arise, will give libraries, museums, schools and churches also a better resurrection.

The aggregate of the Roman Catholic losses in churches and schools seems to have been a little short of $1,500,000; and no mention is made of any insurance. The aggregate actual losses of the various Protestant denominations, after deducting all the insurance which will be received, is about $1,500,000. The various denominations suffered not according to their relative strength in Chicago, but according to the property which they happened to have in the compact business part of the city and on the North Side. The Catholics lost their cathedral, several convents, and many of their best churches and schools. The Methodists also lost very heavily in their branch Book Concern, their Church Block — which was a business house embracing a free church building — and the property of Garrett Biblical Institute, and churches, in all amount-

UNITY AND NEW ENGLAND CHURCHES.

ing to not much less than half a million dollars. The Presbyterians also lost heavily in several elegant churches worth at least $350,000. The Episcopalians lost about $350,000, the Unitarians $175,000, and the Universalists about $80,000. The Baptists, fortunately, with their valuable University property and their best churches, escaped the fire, though their loss was not less than $100,000. Others swell the aggregate to the sum above mentioned. Three millions of dollars devoted to religious uses swept out of existence in twenty-four hours! And this, too, contributed voluntarily by men and women now for the most part impoverished! Many of them now doubt whether they will ever again be able to make another donation for such a purpose.

Is not the church a solidarity? Is it not the mother of democracy and self government? Has not Christianity produced the marvellous sympathy and aid which came from all parts of the world before the flames had completed their work, and continue to come in a steady stream? If not, it is somewhat marvellous that this aid comes only from Christendom, and that it makes such a liberal use of the pulpit and Christian press.

But shall Christians aid Chicago and not directly help the brotherhood to maintain the same cause which inspires them with charity? This might be deemed amiable; it could scarcely be called wise.

But we have no fear for the future of the schools and churches of Chicago. Even if left to themselves, with no aid from abroad, the half million of people that will soon fill these streets and dwell in this reconstructed metropolis will see to it that ample provision is made for intellectual and religious culture; but it will be accomplished slowly and with singular difficulties, and not without much serious loss, unless the community of Christendom proves in this emergency something more than an abstract theory or a vapid sentimentalism. *E. O. Haven.*

INSTITUTIONS OF ART, SCIENCE, LITERATURE.

THE loss to Chicago in places of amusement, libraries, and art-galleries, both public and private, will be realized much more keenly in the future than at present. The public mind is just now too closely occupied with the computation and restoration of the material values of trade and commerce, to give much thought to æsthetic losses. These once regulated, the loss of the latter will make itself apparent. To make any computation of the number of books, pictures, statues, and articles of costly ornament destroyed, is simply impossible. It could only be accomplished by personal reports from every one of the thousands of sufferers who were driven from their homes in the South and North Divisions. An approximate idea, however, may be formed, when it is considered that nearly 30,000 houses were burned, and that many of them, on the avenues of the South Division and on the lake front of the North Division, were among the most elegant in the city and occupied by citizens whose wealth and culture had combined in the accumulation of rare treasures of literature and art.

The chief places of amusement destroyed in the city were Crosby's Opera House, Hooley's Opera House, McVicker's Theatre, the Dearborn Theatre, and Wood's Museum. The last four had just been re-fitted and re-ornamented, and opened for the regular fall season; while Crosby's Opera House was to have been opened on Monday evening, October 9th, the second night of the fire, by the well-known Theodore Thomas' Orchestral Combination. During the winter of 1870, Mr. Crosby had hesitated for some time whether to continue in the amusement business, and had even employed his architect to draw plans for changing the auditorium into commercial offices. The persuasion of friends, however, and the brilliant operatic and otherwise musical prospects for the season of 1871-'72, induced him to abandon the idea of change. Early in the summer the house was closed and the work of adornment commenced. Eighty thousand dollars were expended in seating, upholstery, frescoing, painting, and gilding, in luxurious carpets, superb bronzes, and costly mirrors. It was finished on Saturday, October 7th; and when, on Sunday evening, October 8th — only an hour or two before the fire commenced — the house was lit up that its effect might be seen under gaslight, not one of the few who were present but pronounced it to be the most gorgeous auditorium in America. A few hours after, when Theodore Thomas and his Orchestra arrived, a pile of smoking bricks, stones, and iron, strewn in wild confusion, was all that was left of this beautiful temple of art. It was formally dedicated to art in April, 1865; and during the six years of its existence had been the *locus in quo* of some of the most memorable seasons of English, French, German, and Italian opera, Chicago ever enjoyed. It were useless now to consider what we should have enjoyed in that brilliant auditorium, the nights of Nilsson and Parepa and Thomas and the long array of concerts during the coming winter; but the memories of the past will always be pleasant.

McVicker's Theatre had also been not only ornamented anew, but completely remodelled. Nothing remained of the old theatre but the outside walls, and these were raised an additional story by means of a lofty Mansard roof. The entire interior of the theatre was removed, and a new one substituted upon an entirely different model. There are other theatres in the country more brilliant, but in point of ventilation, acoustics, sight, and general convenience, and especially in the mechanical workings of the stage, it was superior to all. It had been in operation but a few weeks when the fire occurred, having opened to "stock business" in the most successful manner. Mr. Jefferson (Rip Van Winkle) was to have commenced a season on October 9th, and, like Mr. Thomas, arrived here just in time to witness the destruction of the theatre.

Hooley's Opera House, as our readers will remember, was constructed by remodelling the old Bryan Hall, which, prior to the erection of Farwell Hall, and after Metropolitan Hall had gone into disuse, was the *locale* of nearly all the concerts in the city — notably those of the Philharmonic Society, which for many years were the fashionable rage. The building was in no respect an opera house, although, like many others in the country, it had been dignified with this high-sounding name. Mr. Hooley, a gentleman of taste, and great wealth, much of which had been acquired in the business of Ethiopian minstrelsy, purchased the Bryan Hall property and converted it into a theatre, which, during the first year of its existence, was devoted to burnt-cork minstrelsy. Chicago, however, could not support two places of this kind; and during the summer, the house was refitted, the stage enlarged and thoroughly equipped with scenic and mechanical appliances, and in September it was regularly opened as a comedy theatre, under the management of Mr. Frank Aiken, who, a month or two later, associated with himself Mr. Frank Lawlor, and leased the building for five years. It had been in operation but a few weeks when the fire swept it away.

Unlike Hooley's Opera House, the Dearborn Theatre first opened as a dramatic house, under the management of Mr. Frank Aiken, who after a few months took the management of Wood's Museum. The Dearborn then changed colors, and was, up to the time of its destruction, known as the home of the Dearborn Minstrels, under the management of Messrs. Brant & Van Fleet. It was the most elegant minstrel hall in the United States, and possessed what none other can boast — a thoroughly appointed theatrical stage, capable of bringing out the most elaborate scenic spectacles.

Wood's Museum — which combined the attractions of a theatrical stage and curiosity department — was one of the old established institutions of the city. During its long existence, it had met with many vicissitudes, and was rapidly going from worse to worse under different managers, when Colonel Wood, who for many years had been associated with Barnum, and was a master of the "outs and ins" of "show business," assumed the management, and for many years carried it on prosperously. Two or three years since, he retired to his large stock farm at Adrian, Michigan; and Mr. Aiken, to whom we have already alluded, took the management, under a lease from Judge Fuller. It did not succeed, however, under the new management, and Mr. Aiken retired. Once more Colonel Wood was induced to step in. He completely refitted it, enlarged the Curiosity Department, and had just opened with an entirely new theatrical company under the management of Mr. J. S. Langrishe, when it was burned. The Curiosity Department, although large, possessed little of real value. The paintings were, without exception, worthless daubs. The geological cabinet was small; also the cabinet of shells. The collection of birds and insects, however, which formerly belonged to the old St. Louis Museum, was a very choice one; and in addition to these the Museum was in possession of the monstrous saurian unearthed in Alabama some years ago by Dr. Koch.

In addition to these regularly organized places of amusement, three public halls were burned in the South Division — Farwell, Metropolitan, and Crosby's Music Hall; and Uhlich's and North Market Halls, and the German House, in the North Division. Of these, Farwell Hall — the home of the Young Men's Christian Association — was the largest and much the most elaborate. Its seating capacity was for 3,200 persons; and its adornments were of the most elegant description. Metropolitan Hall, latterly known as Library Hall, was an old structure, and was mostly used for lectures and the meetings of the Young Men's Library Association. The Music Hall was on the State Street side of the Crosby Opera House property, and was a sort of tender to that house, taking the smaller concerts and now and then billiard and sparring matches, which were somewhat undignified for a full-blown temple of art. Uhlich's and North Market Halls were both small, and were the respective homes of the Germania and Concordia Mænnerchors, before these two organizations consolidated. The German House was known to but few Americans, but to the Germans it was specially dear as the home of the German drama. We had almost forgotten to mention the Turner Hall, the home of the North Side Turn-Vereins, and on Sabbath evenings devoted to Gambrinus and Polyhymnia in about equal parts.

To replace the opera houses, theatres, and halls, as they were before the fire, would probably involve an outlay of between two and three million dollars. Our managers, not a whit discouraged by their severe losses, are already preparing to build again. Mr. Crosby has decided to build an opera house again on the old site. Mr. Hooley will rebuild his theatre on Clark Street, commencing in the spring; and has also leased the Hadduck property on the northeast corner of Monroe Street and Wabash Avenue, where he will erect a grand opera house during another year. Mr. McVicker has also decided to rebuild his theatre on the old site. Colonel Wood has not yet decided upon anything definite. Messrs. Brant and Van Fleet will restore the Dearborn Theatre, although the site is not yet determined upon. As matters look at present, we shall have to skip one winter of amusements, contenting ourselves with our whist-packs and home pianos and social gatherings, and resume in the old places, in the winter of 1872-'73, with an appetite for amusements all the sharper for the long abstinence.

The principal public galleries of paintings were three in number, viz., the Opera House, Academy of Design, and Historical Society's collections. The paintings in the Opera House Gallery had remained without any important change as they were at the last annual reception in the winter of 1870. The most noted picture in the Gallery was Bierstadt's "Yo Semite Valley," the personal property of Mr. Albert Crosby, which had been in the Gallery many years and had become an old

THE TRIBUNE BUILDING.

familiar friend to every lover of art in the city. Nearly every picture in this collection was saved, through the energy of the Superintendent, Mr. Aitken; and they are now in Boston on exhibition as "relics" of the fire. The managers of the Academy of Design were not so fortunate. The Gallery was a large one, containing some two hundred and fifty or three hundred pictures, nearly all of which were choice. Rothermel's large historical painting of the Battle of Gettysburg was on exhibition at the time of the fire, and was saved; also some pictures by Bierstadt and the Harts, and a large family group—painted by Mr. Pine, the Chicago artist. But a considerable number were lost, as the artists had no means of carrying them away. The Academy included within its province not only the exhibition of works of art, but also the teaching of its principles and practice; and one of its schools, the Antique, had been most liberally provided, by the munificent liberality of Hon. J. Y. Scammon, with a superb collection of casts from the most celebrated antiques, selected in Rome, by Volk, the Sculptor. All of these were destroyed. The larger number of the artists of the city had studios in this building. Two or three of them succeeded in saving a few pictures, but the most of them were involved in the common ruin. The collection at the rooms of the Historical Society was known as the Healey Collection, and was composed, with the exception of Couture's masterly picture, "The Prodigal Son," of that eminent artist's works. It consisted mainly of portraits and groups, among them "Webster before the Senate replying to Hayne," "Franklin before the Court of France," portraits of Clay, Webster, Louis Phillippe, Marshal Soult, Miss Sneyd the English belle, Calhoun, and several portraits of the founders and officers of the Society.

Of the private galleries in the city, it is impossible to speak in any detail. Messrs. Scammon, Johnson, Arnold, Sheldon, McCagg, and others, had valuable collections which were irrecoverably lost. Among other works of art lost by Mr. McCagg, were Powers's fine Statue of Pocahontas and Healey's historical picture of the Hampton Roads Conference.

The principal scientific institution of Chicago was the Academy of Sciences, situated on the South Side, and enclosed in walls supposed to be fireproof. Within were contained the results of many expeditions in distant seas and distant lands. The large collection of Invertebrates, comprised in ten thousand alcoholic jars, each jar containing from eight to ten specimens, made by Wilkes, Ringold, and other navigators, originally consigned to the custody of the Smithsonian Institution, but transferred here for study and elucidation by Dr. Stimpson; his own MSS., prepared for publication, and illustrated by numerous drawings and engravings, descriptive of the fauna of the Japan Expedition; the Cooper collection of shells, one of the best in the country, and purchased by Mr. George Walker; the library of conchology, embracing the best works on that science, also secured by the munificence of the same individual; the collection of the game birds of America, made by the Audubon Club, together with a copy of Audubon's magnificently illustrated work; an almost complete collection of the mammals and birds of the continent and the most characteristic foreign specimens; two skeletons of the mastodon, besides the crania of many other extinct forms; a cabinet of minerals peculiarly rich in crystalline specimens, secured through the exertions of Mr. Chesbrough; a magnificent collection of Mexican antiquities, the gift of Mr. Scammon; a large collection of the implements of the mound-builders, together with an elaborate MS. by Colonel Foster, descriptive of the same; the collections of Robert Kennicott in the Arctic Regions, which served as the foundation of the Museum; the botanical collections of Dr. Scammon, made during his life-time, embracing many specimens of plants which now have nearly disappeared from their former habitats; the collections of Dr. Veille on the plains and in the mountains, embracing years of toil and active exploration; — these are among the treasures offered up in the great holocaust of fire

Chicago had no great public libraries, as compared with the libraries of New York, Boston, and other Eastern cities. The energies of her citizens, as in all young places, have been devoted to the establishment of trade and commerce, the organization and equipment of railroad and steamboat lines, and the devising of means to conduct the exchanges of the vast Northwest with the seaboard. Material growth always comes first; and the luxuries of literature and art only follow after the accumulation of wealth, and result from culture, which in its turn results from the leisure which wealth gives.

And yet Chicago was not without libraries prior to the fire, which were accumulated for the public benefit. The Young Men's Library numbered 20,000 volumes, of a rather heterogeneous character, and principally noticeable for a complete set of the British Patent-Office Reports — which, by-the-bye, have proved, notwithstanding their importance to the mechanical classes, both a literary and financial elephant of the most unmanageable description. The only striking result of this rather costly gift from the English Government was the entail of a debt, which hung upon the Association like an incubus, and was tenderly handed down from one administration to another, constantly growing with the handling. But very few of the books were saved, and the salvage is scattered far and wide.

The library of the Historical Society was one of great historical value, and embraced 17,500 bound volumes, 145,000 pamphlets, a large collection of manuscripts, and several complete newspaper files. Incidentally we may tsate that the Society also possessed the original draft of the Emancipation Proclamation of President Lincoln. The importance of this library cannot be too highly estimated. Its volumes represented the documentary history, not only of Chicago, but also of the Northwest; and what adds to the weight of the disaster is the fact that the largest part of this loss is total. It will be next to impossible to duplicate any considerable portion of it. Since the fire, the members of the Society have met and elected Rev. Wm. Barry, who was its founder, their Secretary. His untiring skill and patient industry will undoubtedly do much towards the formation of another library, but it must be from small beginnings. It seems to us that it would be eminently proper, as soon as the Society has once more secured rooms, to seek first to restore as far as possible the history of Chicago. This may be accomplished in part by correspondence with similar institutions in other States, many of which may have duplicate copies of works pertaining to Chicago; by manuscript donations from our older settlers, covering their personal reminiscences; and by an urgent appeal to the public at large to donate whatever pamphlets, documents and books they may have, concerned with our history as a city. Above all, this one plan should be kept steadily in view for the present: viz., the restoration of the history of Chicago. To attempt the history of the Northwest or of the United States would only involve the members in useless expense and the library in chaotic confusion. The fire, by consuming a good deal of chaff, has given the Society a golden opportunity to establish a systematic library of reference.

The library of the Academy of Sciences numbered 5,000 volumes, devoted to the specialties of that association. The Young Men's Christian Association during the past two or three years had accumulated 10,000 volumes, mostly of a theological character. The Union Catholic Library, although commenced quite recently, numbered 5,000 volumes, mostly of a sectarian character. The Franklin Library, which pertained to the "Art preservative of arts," was organized two or three years since by a printer, and had already reached the handsome number of 3,000 volumes, many of which were exceedingly old and rare. Cobb's Library, on Washington Street near State, was a circulating library numbering about 5,000 volumes. Placing the libraries of smaller associations at 10,000 vol-

INSTITUTIONS OF ART, SCIENCE, LITERATURE.

umes, we have in all a loss of over 100,000 volumes in our public libraries.

It is impossible to speak with any certainty of the loss of private libraries or the number of works destroyed. Horace White, Esq., the editor of the *Chicago Tribune*, lost a valuable political library; likewise Hon. I. N. Arnold. Perry Smith, Geo. L. Dunlap, Obadiah Jackson, and numerous other residents of the North Division, lost large and valuable miscellaneous libraries. E. B. McCagg lost one of the finest philological libraries in the United States, and J. Y. Scammon one of the most extensive collections of Swedenborgian works in the country. When we consider that there is not a house in the city, whose occupants make any pretensions to taste, which did not have its library, large or small, and not a hovel so poor but that some book could be found in it, we can form some slight idea of the wide-spread destruction of literature in our homes alone. Fifteen or twenty clergymen were burned out, and their libraries in most cases were a total loss. The sanitary department has a list of nearly two hundred physicians who were burned out. Many, if not most, of these, lost their offices, instruments, and books; and Judge J. M. Wilson reckons the number of lawyers whose libraries were burned, at five hundred. It is probably a fair estimate to set the loss of theological, medical and law libraries alone at half a million dollars; while the accumulations in the bookstores would swell this amount into the millions.

It may be considered absurd to attempt to form any estimate of the number of books destroyed by the fire, but estimating moderately we should be inclined to think that it would reach between two and three millions — a literary holocaust compared with which the destruction of the Alexandrian and Strasburg libraries seems insignificant.

Readers of THE LAKESIDE will hardly need to be reminded of the number or the character of the great bookstores of Chicago. The English press, in commenting upon the buildings, invariably speak of the stores of Booksellers' Row, on State Street, as the finest in the world. In convenience of arrangement, elegance of finish, and variety of stock, they were unrivalled. Messrs. S. C. Griggs & Co., in addition to a full stock of the books of the day and educational works, had given much attention to books of a higher class; and their stock included many of the richly illustrated foreign works. Their loss in stock and fixtures was about $225,000; of which about one-half is insured. The Western News Company dealt largely in newspapers and periodicals, and yet always kept on hand a large stock of the current books of the market. Their loss on stock was about $200,000, on which there is an insurance of $160,000. W. B. Keen, Cooke & Co., in addition to their large stock of books, always kept a full line of stationery. Their loss was about $175,000; insured for $130,000. Cobb, Andrews & Co. lost $80,000, insurance $66,000; Woodworth, Ainsworth & Co., $8,000, insurance $6,000; the agency of A. S. Barnes & Co., of New York, $40,000, insurance $39,000; Hadley Brothers, $75,000, insurance in full; and Ivison, Blakeman, Taylor & Co., $15,000, fully insured.

The list of newspapers and magazine offices burned out is a formidable one. Not having a reference at hand, we append the list from memory:

DAILY PAPERS IN ENGLISH.—Tribune, Times, Republican, Journal, Post, and Mail.—6.

DAILIES AND WEEKLIES (foreign).—Augustana, Union, Die Freie Presse, Fremad, Gamla och Nya, Staats Zeitung, Volks' Zeitung, Amerikanische Farmer, Missionaren, Nya Verden, Landewerth, Haus Freund, Die Deutsche Arbeiter, Catholische Wochenblatt, Svenska Amerikanaren, Tuxbruder, Skandinavien, and Westliche Unterhaltungs Blaater.—19.

JUVENILE PUBLICATIONS.—Little Men, Young Pilot, Young Folks' Rural, Young Messenger, Bright Side, Our Boys, Little Corporal, Child's Paper, Child's World, Young Reaper, Amateur's Guide, Youth's Cabinet, Young Hero, Scholar, and Little Folks.—15.

AGRICULTURAL.—Western Rural and Prairie Farmer.—2.

RELIGIOUS WEEKLIES.—Western Catholic, Sunday-School Helper, New Covenant, Interior, Catholic Weekly, Present Age, Choir, Northwestern Christian Advocate, Song Festival, Sunday-School Teacher, Lyceum Banner, Heavenly Tidings, Standard, Progress, Advance, Restitution, Religio-Philosophical Journal, and Bethel Banner.—18.

MONTHLY MAGAZINES.—LAKESIDE MONTHLY, Arts, American Builder, Examiner, Bureau, Manford's Magazine, Chicago Magazine of Fashion, Congregational Review, Homœopathic Magazine, Medical Times, Journal of Microscopy, Lens, Art Review, Bench and Bar, Pharmacist, Medical Examiner, Mystic Star, and School Master.—18.

BUSINESS PERIODICALS.—Chicago Advertiser, Board of Trade Report, Chicago Collector, Commercial Bulletin, Commercial Express, Dry Goods Price List, Journal of Commerce, Railway Review, Railroad Gazette, Commercial Report and Market Review, Northwestern Review, Real Estate and Building Journal, Chicago Ledger, Chicago Mercantile Journal, Insurance Chronicle, Detector, Land Owner, Spectator, Western Railway Guide, Rand & McNally's Railway Guide, Bryant & Chase's Review, and Druggists' Price Current.—22.

MISCELLANEOUS.—Bouquet Programme, Balance, Lorgnette, Chicago Democrat, Home Journal, Happy Hours, Legal News, Chicago Cynosure, Evening Lamp, Everybody's Paper, Gem of the West, Soldiers' Friend, Home Circle and Temperance Oracle, Life Boat, National Prohibitionist, Chicago Weekly, Family Circle, Herald, Independent, Mechanic and Inventor, National, People's Weekly, Reporter, Workingman's Advocate, Daily Law Record, Inside Track, Western Odd Fellow, and Voice of Masonry.—28.

Total number of publications burned out, 128.

G. P. Upton.

PART V.—THE FUTURE.

WHAT REMAINS.

THE sensations of that committee of intelligent gentlemen from Boston, on their recent visit to our city, may be taken as representative. They trailed through the long avenues of ruin, saw a desolation so complete that neither shrub nor roof, and scarcely an exceptional wall, remained — three thousand acres sown with ashes; and their impression was frankly given that Chicago was blotted out, that there was no nucleus around which to build, that if ever reconstructed only the outside demand for a city must be consulted, for there was absolutely nothing left inside to justify restoration. Our ruins challenge such a verdict. A gentleman of large interests in the city invited them to drive with him. He conveyed them to Lake View, beyond Lincoln Park, and swept them over the broad expanse of the West Side, whose thoroughfares are crammed as though for a holiday. Their eyes picked up the magnificent churches, the miles of homes of every order, the great lumber yards stretching far south and west, the Stock Yards with their clatter of hoofs and jostle of horns, the business pushing south along the avenues, past Douglas Place to the Boulevards, and they exclaimed, "You have no need of rebuilding. You have now standing one of the busiest, most populous cities of the nation." These counter impressions are inevitable. Desolation unprecedented, thrift unprecedented, destruction and useful power, lie side by side. The black patch is the blackest and the bright patch the brightest. Between live Chicago and dead Chicago there is no purgatorial mediation, no twilight of convalescence.

These sensations represent the feelings of the people. On Tuesday morning after the fire, all was lost. To-day, to the sanguine, the opportunities afforded for improvement in reconstruction have made a gain of the loss. It has been estimated that $400,000,000 of property and 200,000 people were undisturbed in their residences. The vast lumber interest, on which we are to depend so largely for material, was unharmed. The packing houses, representatives of Chicago commerce, were not singed. The Stock Yards, marvels in extent and perfection, were left to serve the world's provision market. Only five of the grain elevators out of the seventeen which the city contained were destroyed.

Though more miles of sidewalk have been burned than would reach from the Lake to the Mississippi, yet twice that amount remains. The three tunnels, which mark an era in engineering skill, giving us connection with fresh water under the lake, and roadways that are fire-proof, uniting our three-sectioned city, are all intact. Highways, so long a desiderata of our rapid growth, with their accompanying sewerage, water, and gas, are without serious damage. The railways still point their unintermitting tide to this focus. The business which energy and capital have catered for throughout the West and Northwest, with hardly an exception remained true to its habit. The rivers are very few whose source and mouth you can transpose as our engineers did the Chicago River. It is a poor satisfaction that we have our ruins left, without ivy or owl or bat, as vieing with the curiosities of the world.

Fire chiefly destroyed material things, not character—though there were a few mental and moral shaving piles that burned up. That night, when the social and the civil framework were shattered, bloody riot and chaotic law-breaking did not seize our masses. Calmness, earnest resignation and heroism stood out to dignify destruction. Even fire is better than some emasculating corruption which saps the integrity of the inhabitants.

It is the champion fire. That stands in history. The best time upon record that fire ever made— four and a half miles in eighteen hours. Chicago has not remaining the pusillanimity of having been slain by an insignificant catastrophe, but by a conflagration that would have prostrated London or New York. She has been reminded by a benevolence which is the most majestic feature of the age, that her commercial and social relations with the whole world still stand.

Like the bed of some mighty river suddenly licked dry, the fountain and the streamlets and the clouds remain. The channel is clear. All agencies are busy filling its banks again. The men remain—those selected for forty years, out of all the nations on the earth, as best fitted for this mercurial life. Compared with the laws that work to assort such an army, and the expense of pain and purse to root them here, the burned buildings are but rubbish and twopence. The only cities that are built of marble and mortar are cemeteries and mausoleums. A city means men and women.

How much folly and selfishness we have left, will be displayed in the scrabble to locate official and business centres. It has been supposed that the government and municipal buildings were on wheels, and that the strongest team of selfish influence would determine their unloading. We trust that all greed so monstrous perished in the fire without insurance. Aside from one hypochondriac maiden whom the sudden fright restored, we have heard of no credits entered up to the fire of diseases cured. Our friend with the crutches did not lose his rheumatism with his supports, and the cough of our consumptive neighbor was better protected than were greenbacks in the safes. Fires would be useful if they would burn up only nuisances, diseases, weaknesses and wood. If that enemy of childhood could have caught the *fever* heat and *scarlet* color from the occasion, and made it a cremation, all infanthood would have paid the insurance with a smile. The man who dug down to find whether the mortgage was burned off with the buildings, discovered that mortgages are the only fire-proof structures you can place upon a lot.

All the bores and scolds, most of the drunkards and thieves, are slightly disarranged, but are eddying to their centres. It is singular that when society takes to itself wings and flies away, it will fly back and alight, like a migratory bird, in its old locality.

There remains as the delicate and permanent crystal precipitated by this disaster, an exquisite and lustrous gratitude in every Chicago heart. Such a remnant is like a mountain clarified and chemicalized to a diamond. It shall be the jewel in the casket of the New Chicago. We confidently believe that in the records of the work of the " Relief and Aid Society" and of tributary and supplementary charities, a monument of system, judicious expenditure and integrity will be built, which will be a credit to the city and a model for the world.

William Alvin Bartlett.

NEW CHICAGO.

IN the opening paper of this number we have shown how forbidding was the aspect of the original site of Chicago, and what a series of public works were executed to make it one of the most attractive cities in the Union. So overpowering was the commercial necessity that here should be a great *entrepot*, that one would have been constructed, even if the ground had had to be reclaimed from Lake Michigan. The same causes which led to this wonderful development, still exist in full force. The resources of Chicago are but slightly impaired. Her geographical position is on the water-shed between two great systems of inland navigation, the St. Lawrence and the Mississippi, by which she can communicate with the Atlantic and the Gulf of Mexico. The navigable waters of these river systems exceed 12,000 miles, and they afford a transportation which for cheapness can never be superceded by any artificial mode of conveyance. The differences of climate, soil, and products along the line of these two river systems, lie at the foundation of the extensive exchanges which must for all time be maintained between regions thus widely separated. Chicago is also the centre of a network of railways which have cost not less than $300,000,000. Not a mile of track will be abandoned in consequence of the fire; nor will their transporting capacity be in the least diminished. The proprietors of the great pineries of the North will continue to make use of this port for the sale and transfer of their immense cargoes of lumber so extensively used in the Mississippi Valley, and the beef and pork and breadstuffs of the West will still continue to accumulate here, preparatory to their distribution throughout the markets of the world. Some of our business men who wielded these vast interests, may be compelled to succumb to their misfortunes; but other men with other means will come in to take their places. Capital instinctively flows to the most profitable channels ; it requires no legislation to direct it. When a vessel founders at sea, the waves close over her and the surface almost instantly assumes its wonted aspect. So the void created by this calamity will soon be filled by capital flowing in from other cities the world over. The great volume of commerce will continue to move in its accustomed channels. There will be found men enough and means enough for all its requirements.

It is a singular fact in political economy, that a nation whose government is stable and whose laws are judicious and well administered, rapidly recovers from apparently overwhelming misfortune. The Northern States are far richer to-day than before the Rebellion. England rapidly recovered from the immense drain upon her resources during her continental wars, and for half a century has been the richest kingdom in Christendom; and France bears up wonderfully under the terrible defeats inflicted upon her by Prussia. Ten years, it is estimated, is sufficient for a nation to recuperate from the effects of the most desolating war; and five years, we predict, will be sufficient to obliterate from Chicago all traces of the Great Conflagration. Taught by this terrible example, her people will realize the necessity, for the first time in her history, of discarding inflammable materials in the construction of external walls. Without the enforcement of such a policy, insurance will demand exorbitant rates, capital will seek safer investments, and business men will live in constant dread of wide-spread conflagrations. It will be found that no policy could be adopted more fatal to the permanent prosperity of the city, than to allow the burnt district to be rebuilt in the same reckless and improvident manner as before the fire. If the greed of speculators, in this respect, overmasters the judicious public sentiment, let the authority of the Legislature be invoked. We have yet two considerable cities left — one on the South Side and one on the West; but both of them are liable to the same visitation which reduced to ashes the central portion and the Northern Division.

We believe, then, that in this contest — for it has already assumed that position — the judicious public sentiment will triumph; and instead of long streets of shanties, we shall have substantial tenements of brick and stone.

As the burnt districts of London, Moscow, and New York rose from their ashes more substantially built, more beautifully adorned, and better adapted to the wants of commerce, so will it be with the burnt district of Chicago. Already from out the depths of her desolation she proclaims as her motto — " RESURGAM."

J. W. Foster.

SUPPLEMENTARY.

THE FIRES OF HISTORY.

VIEWED from the standpoint of the Chicago fire, the great fires of history are few and far between. The magnitude of the present calamity, in respect of area, value of property destroyed, number of people rendered homeless, and consequent extent of suffering entailed, is such that most of those conflagrations of the past which are deemed of sufficient importance to find a place upon the page of history are dwarfed by comparison. The situation of Chicago, its commercial importance, and intimate connection with all the great interests, not only of the West, but of the New World itself, render its destruction probably more noticeable and startling, and its results more widely felt, than those of any other similar calamity on record. Chicago was, and is, one of the wonders of the world. The unparalleled rapidity of its growth — springing in the brief space of thirty years from a mere hamlet to an immense commercial metropolis the third in size of the Union — has awakened the wonder and admiration of the world; spreading its fame to the remotest corner of civilized life, not only as the proudest manifestation of the concentration of all Anglo-Saxon energy and enterprise, but also as the shining type of the progress of the Nineteenth century. Hence its loss has aroused the sympathy of mankind to an extent unequalled in the annals of profane history, and rendered this awful 8th and 9th of October memorable for all time. Not even the Franco-German war has so marked this year of 1871 as the great Chicago fire, which henceforth creates a new starting point for the memories of the rising generation.

But, however the magnitude of this calamity may have dwarfed out of sight many of those which were heretofore considered among the great fires of the past, there are still left many ineffaceable spots upon the tablets of history, where this most destructive of the elements has scorched its record upon the ages, here and there, at long intervals, marking in flame the story of human suffering wrought by man's destructiveness, Divine vengeance, or the inevitable accident common to all human affairs.

The earliest recorded fire is the destruction of Sodom and Gomorrah, Admah and Zeboim, the "cities of the plain," now slumbering eternally beneath the Dead Sea waters, a mark to all earthly generations of the wrath of an offended Deity. The burning of these cities, recorded only in Holy Writ, took place about the year 1897, B.C., and is only known as a great fact of the world's history, all the details being forever lost.

Sardis, the once famous capital of Lydia in Asia Minor, the residence of Crsœus of fabled wealth, the "Hyde" of Homer, and seat of one of the seven churches mentioned in the Book of Revelations, was burned by the Ionians and Athenians in the year 504, B. C., its destruction resulting in the famous wars of the Greeks and Persians, which culminated some twenty-four years later in the defeat of Xerxes the Great, whose chief motive for his Greek campaign is said to have been his indignation at the wanton destruction of this wealthy and beautiful city.

The next great flame of history which startled the ancient world, was the burning of the magnificent temple of Diana at Ephesus, in the year 356, B. C. This temple was one of the "Seven Wonders of the World." It was 425 feet in length and 220 feet high — its roof of cedar resting upon a marble entablature and supported by 128 columns, 60 feet in height, each the gift of a king. It contained an ivory statue of Diana, the master-pieces of the most eminent artists, and enormous wealth of ornamentation, chiefly of the precious metals. It was fired by one Erostratus, otherwise unknown to fame, whose only motive for the act was expressed in his dying words, "A yearning for immortality"; an immortality of infamy which the deed secured in spite of Grecian enactments by which his countrymen strove to bury even his name in oblivion. As the flames of the temple ascended to heaven, a flaming scourge of humanity descended upon earth in the person of Alexander the Great, whose birth on that same night was heralded by the triumph of the fiery element, as the death of Napoleon was, in later years, by the war of the elements of the air.

Twenty-eight years later, in the year 328, B. C., this same Alexander, in a drunken frolic, and at the behest of a courtesan, fired the palace of Persepolis, which was consumed, with a large portion of the city, startling the world with horror at the results of the twin vices of drunkenness and sensuality.

Thus Divine vengeance destroyed the cities of the plain — human wrath and vengeance the piled wealth of Sardis — a foolish yearning for notoriety Diana's gorgeous temple, and wine and women the beautiful palace and city of Persepolis.

But none of these conflagrations so shook the world and so deeply burned their memory upon the pages of history, as did that of Rome in the year 69. This act has generally been attributed to Nero, in the tenth year of whose reign it occurred. By some historians, however, it was attributed to the Christians, and by others to a sect of so-called Galilaeans, followers of Judas the Gaulonite. The story of Nero's guilt, and of his "fiddling while Rome was burning," is now generally considered a myth, so unreliable and conflicting are the statements of historians; and the question of the authorship of the calamity is involved in doubt which can never be cleared away. The conflagration raged for eight days, totally destroying three of the fourteen districts of the city, and leaving only a few half-ruined houses standing in seven others, only four districts remaining unharmed. In this destruction perished an immense treasure of Greek and Roman art — trophies of their wars — and temples and costly palaces innumerable. Rome was then but little past the zenith of her power and glory. The city must have contained a population of 2,000,000, and was crowded with the captured and imported wealth of all nations. She was then the metropolis of the world, and the total destruction of five-sevenths of her entire area must have involved incalculable loss and untold misery to her teeming population, though of the details of loss and suffering history preserves no record. The result of the fire, however, was in the end advantageous to the city itself, since it was immediately rebuilt in far better style, of more durable materials, and upon a more regular plan. Heeding the lesson of the conflagration, the Emperor prohibited the use of wood in its reconstruction.

The next year after the burning of Rome — in the year 70 — occurred the destruction of Jerusalem by Titus, in which the magnificent temple of the Jews, together with a large portion of the city, was given to the flames, in spite of the frantic efforts of Titus himself to stay the wanton destruction. The wealth of the city was enormous, and its size may be appreciated from the fact that, according to Josephus, 1,100,000 people perished in its siege and destruction. As almost the entire Jewish race was assembled in the city to celebrate the feast of unleavened bread when all egress was cut off by the besieging army, it may well be believed that the loss of life from the conflagration itself, aside from the slaughter by the Romans, must have been such as the world never saw before or since. Indeed the historian relates that 6,000 people, men, women, and children, were burned in a single building in which they had sought refuge.

In the year 642 was burned, by order of the Caliph Omar, the Alexandrian Library, the most enormous collection of books the world has ever seen, containing at one time, according to some writers 400,000, according to others 700,000 volumes. The Caliph's reason for its destruction was curious enough. "If," said he, "these Greek books agree with the Koran, they are useless; if not, they should be destroyed," — and accordingly, without stopping to settle the question, the torch was applied, and the stored wealth of classic lore, the work of men's brains for ages, and which had consumed centuries in their collection, went up to heaven in smoke and flame, and in their destruction were forever lost the works of some of the world's greatest minds ; and many an author of once towering fame, was by a single fire consigned to oblivion.

Descending to more modern times, we find the first really great fire on record to be that of London, in the year 1666. Like most large cities, London has had more than one contest with the fire fiend. In the year 61, it was burned by the Britons; in the years 893, 1077, 1086, 1132, and 1136, it was nearly consumed. At these times, however, it was but an inconsiderable city, its population in 1141 being only 40,000. The fire of 1666 broke out on September 3d, in a baker's shop, and owing to the narrow streets, wooden buildings, an extremely dry season, and a violent east wind blowing at the time, spread so rapidly that it resisted all efforts to extinguish it. Four days and nights it raged incessantly, and was only checked at last by the free use of gunpowder, blowing up whole blocks in the line of its path. Five-sixths of the entire city within the walls was destroyed, the conflagration extending over an area of more than 400 acres, and destroying 400 streets and 13,000 houses. King Charles II. and his brother the Duke of York — afterwards James II.— were on the scene in person, directing the efforts of the firemen, and doing yeoman's service in fighting the flames. In its incidents and results, this fire was more similar to that of Chicago than any other on record. The frightened people were driven in crowds from street to street, and from one refuge to another, families being separated, parents and children, husbands and wives, seeking each other in vain, and finally the whole panic-stricken multitude were driven to sleep in the fields beyond the city, in the midst of a shower of rain. The misery and suffering of rich and poor alike were immense. The public storehouses were thrown open, and thousands were fed by charity. Parliament immediately voted a levy of £1,800,000 to relieve the necessities of the suffering. And as in the present case, one of the first great questions which agitated the public mind was that of the titles to real estate, and Parliament was forced to appoint commissioners to decide all questions arising from the loss of deeds and records.

The results, however, as is generally the case in such calamities, was in the end beneficial. The city was, within four years, rebuilt in far better style. Wooden material, which before had been almost universally used in building, was now absolutely prohibited; the streets were made wider and more regular, and the whole plan of the city improved; and, best of all, the plague, which for centuries before had periodically ravaged the city, was thereafter unknown.

Constantinople, from its faulty construction and inflammable material, has so frequently been the victim of fire that a conflagration in that city rarely attracts the attention of the world. In 1778 and 1782 large portions of this city were consumed. In 1852, in a single night, seven fires destroyed 3,500 houses; and no longer ago than 1870 a great fire swept away 7,000 of its houses, entailing a loss of £25,000,000 or $125,000,000 of our money ; a loss which in magnitude approaches that of Chicago.

Next to the Great Fire of London, the most shining mark of flame upon the tablets of history was the burning of Moscow, startling as well by its own magnitude and extent of loss and suffering, as by its indirect consequence in the immense privation and loss of human life which it entailed upon the French army. Moscow was nearly consumed by fire in 1536, 1547, and again in 1571, when it was fired in the suburbs by the Tartars, and a large portion of the population perished in the flames. In 1611 it was again partly burnt by the Poles. Some idea of the magnitude of its last conflagration in 1812 may be obtained from the facts that it was then a city as large as Chicago, containing 4,000 stone and 8,000 wooden buildings, with a population of 300,000, and covering an area at that time larger than the city of London, being eight miles in diameter and twenty-four miles in circumference. It was built in four concentric circles, each surrounded by a strong wall. It was the capital and metropolis of the Russian Empire, crowded with the wealth, luxury, and refinement of the great Empire of the North. Prior to its evacuation by the Russian army, its inhabitants were ruthlessly driven out, 100,000 of them to perish in the barren and inhospitable fields, in the most frightful suffering and privation. A long drought had prevailed. A tempest of wind sprang up the day before the fire, as if on purpose to aid in its destruction. The fire engines had been destroyed, and all means of extinguishing the flames cut off. The city was fired in five hundred places, and soon, in spite of the frantic efforts of the French soldiery, became an "ocean of flame." The scenes that transpired in its streets were too horrible for pen to depict. Thirty thousand of the Russian sick and wounded were burned to death, and Napoleon himself almost miraculously escaped. When at last the flame fiend departed, but 200 stone and 500 wooden buildings remained standing. The French army, which left the smoking ruins over 100,000 strong, was nearly annihilated in its retreat. Directly and indirectly, 200,000 human lives were sacrificed by this barbarous act of Rostopchin.

On May 5th, 1842, a fire broke out in the city of Hamburg, which raged for four days, destroying one-third of the entire city. And with this we close the record of the Old World.

On our own continent, the first conflagration of note, and the greatest before that of Chicago, was that of New York city in 1835, which swept the first ward east of Broadway and below Wall Street, destroying 648 stores, the Merchant's Exchange South Dutch Church, and property valued at over $18,000,000.

On July 19th, 1845, New York was again visited by fire, which raged between Broadway, Exchange Place, Broad and Stone Streets, destroying $5,000,000 worth of property.

In Charleston, S. C., on April 27th, 1838, 1.158 buildings were destroyed by fire, over an area of 145 acres.

Pittsburg was visited by flames on April 10th, 1845, her entire business quarter, to the extent of sixty acres and 1,000 buildings, being consumed, at a loss of $5,000,000.

The same year two terrible fires occurred in Quebec, at a month's interval, destroying in all 3,000 buildings and over $8,000,000 worth of property, making a loss in that disastrous year of some $18,000,000 in four conflagrations.

In September, 1848, some twenty-four acres of the city of Albany, containing over 300 buildings, were burned over, the loss being over $3,000,000.

St. Louis, in July, 1849, lost 350 buildings, and property valued at $3,000,000.

San Francisco, from its crowded construction and combustible materials, has been peculiarly subject to fires. Her greatest losses from this cause have been — on December 24th, 1849, $1,000,000; May 4th, 1850, $3,000,000; June 14th, 1850, $3,000,000; May 2d, 1851, $7,000,000, including 2,500 buildings; June 22d, 1851, $2,000,000; making within eighteen months a total loss by fire of $16,000,000, in a city of 30,000 inhabitants, or over $500 for every living soul within her limits.

The greatest single calamity by fire, between the great fire of New York and that of Chicago, was the burning of Portland, Maine, on July 4th, 1866. This conflagration arose from so simple a matter as a firecracker in the hands of a careless boy. A gale of wind was blowing from the south, which carried the flames in spite of every effort, sweeping as with the besom of destruction a space a mile in length and a quarter of a mile in width, and destroying nearly one-half the city, including the business portions. Even gunpowder failed to check the flames, over fifty buildings being blown up in vain. The loss was estimated at over $10,000,000. More than a quarter of the entire population of the city was rendered homeless, and thousands of them lived for weeks in tents and huts, supported by the contributions of money, food, and clothing which poured in from the other cities of the Union, to the value of half a million dollars. It may well be said that the Portland youngster's fire cracker was the costliest one ever fired in America. "Ten cents a bunch," is the usual price; but this one cracker cost Portland $10,000,000.

Egbert Phelps.

SCIENCE OF THE NORTHWESTERN FIRES.

THE comprehensive plan of the "Fire proof" number of THE LAKESIDE would be scarcely complete without some reference to the effects of the great conflagration upon the general conditions of the Earth's surface, and the vegetable and animal forms that exist upon it. Of course such a topic could not be treated exhaustively within the limits of a magazine article; we simply propose to take a brief glance at the subject, and to close with an attempt to show the primary causes of the terrible phenomenon.

It will be necessary, however, in this discussion, to take in with the mind's eye a much larger area than that of the burned district in Chicago. The wholesale devastation of our fair city was but an item in the wide-spread ravages of the fire fiend during the first half of October, 1871. At the time the fairest portion of our city was being laid in ashes, the devouring flames were making havoc almost all over the United States of America. On that fatal night the fires were sweeping over the lumbering regions of Wisconsin, Michigan, and Minnesota, laying bare many thousands of acres of timber land, and burning up every organic substance on a vast range of improved land in those States. And about the same time, New York, Pennsylvania, Indiana, Kansas, Missouri, California, Nevada, and the Rocky Mountain regions, were alike visited by destructive conflagrations. Many scores of thousands of people were rendered homeless, hundreds were killed, and the property accumulations of several years were ruthlessly swept out of existence.

In the chemical and meteorological changes evolved by these fires, the Chicago conflagration really acted but a subordinate part; though immense in itself, it was but small in proportion to the whole.

It is yet too early to make an accurate estimate of the area traversed by the fire in the forests of the Northwestern States. That can only be done after the whole ground has been re-surveyed. But the very lowest estimate we can make places the amount of timbered land actually burned over, at not less than 480,000 acres, of which 200,000 acres are in Michigan. This is equal to 750 square miles of territory, containing the material that would yield a product of 1,800,000,000 feet of lumber for the market, or very nearly as much as Chicago has received during the past two years.

At least an equal extent of other than timbered land was burned over — including what are technically called "clearings," where the trees have been cut down, leaving vast quantities of combustible material, and many hundreds of farms, some of them a long way removed from the lumber regions. The total area of country burned over, wooded and open, cannot be less than one thousand square miles, and is probably very much more than that amount.

And this vast tract of country was completely denuded. The ordinary fire in the woods only burns up the brush, and the boughs of trees, leaving the trunks standing, with a mere char on the outside; they can still be utilized for lumber, provided they are cut down and thrown into the water before the well-known borer has a chance to attack them. But in the fires of last October a large proportion of the trees were burned through to the core, and fell to the ground, little better than attenuated sticks of charcoal. It was a *destroying* fire, that literally burned up, "root and branch," while the fences, hay, buildings, etc., on the farming lands were so completely licked up that not even the ashes were left to indicate the places where they had formerly existed.

It is manifestly impossible to tell exactly the quantities of wood, hay, straw, and other combustibles burned up in those fires. Could we do so, it would be easy to calculate the precise number of pounds of carbon set free in the process; because the science of Chemistry enables us to say, to an ounce, how much of each of the elements enters into the composition of a ton of any named material. Thus, we know that straw and dry pine wood each contain thirty - eight per cent. of carbon, and hay nearly forty - one (40.73) per cent. But we can make a sufficiently close approximation to answer our present purpose. Taking the *minima* of estimated area of country as a basis, the writer has made a careful calculation from averages of the quantities of material destroyed on those areas, and has computed, in a similar way, the products of the combustion in the city of Chicago, with the following conclusions :

As a chemical result of this immense burning, we have not less than three million tons of carbon from the country, and three hundred thousand tons from the city, liberated from its union with other elements, and carried up into the air. Every three pounds of this would take up eight pounds of oxygen, forming eleven pounds of carbonic acid gas. Here we have an addition of twelve million tons of free carbonic acid gas to the quantity already existing in the atmosphere. Knowing as we do how much the conditions of animal and vegetable existence depend upon the constitution of the ærial envelope of our globe, it becomes important to ascertain the extent of disturbance from the normal state, produced by this phenomenon.

The quantity of carbonic acid gas normal to the atmosphere at the present day is estimated to be about one part in two thousand ; the weight will, therefore, be a little less than twenty thousand million tons. Hence its proportion in the atmosphere has been increased by about one part in sixteen hundred. The total weight of atmospheric oxygen being a little over nine million million tons, its proportion has been decreased to the extent of nearly one part in a million. Accepting Liebig's estimate that the annual consumption of oxygen by the lower animals and by combustion is double the quantity consumed by human beings in breathing, we arrive at the astounding result that the oxygen taken up by the Northwestern fires was equal to the amount required to supply the consumption of ten months all over the globe.

So far as we are able to judge, the vegetable kingdom was intended by the Creator to act as an exact counterpoise to the animal world, the former returning to the atmosphere just as much oxygen as is taken by the latter. This does not seem to be the case with carbon, the atmospheric proportion of which appears to have slowly decreased ever since the Carboniferous era. At that time the quantity of carbonic acid gas in the atmosphere was probably three hundred times greater than now, holding in combination one - half of the oxygen, and forming fifteen to twenty per cent. of the total weight of the air (Brogniart estimates seven or eight per cent.). The amount of free carbonic acid gas has diminished, approximately, at the rate of about one part in five thousand each century since then. In this respect, therefore, the Northwestern fires have restored the atmospheric conditions of three hundred years ago.

A glance at the characteristics of the Carboniferous era will enable us to appreciate the importance of this fact. We know that if we replace eight per cent. of the oxygen in the atmosphere of the present day with an equal volume of carbonic acid gas, the mixture is alike fatal to animal life and to combustion. Even the lower orders of animal life could only exist when the atmosphere had been partially cleared of its superabundant carbon. And this was accomplished by the vegetable kingdom, which then flourished with a luxuriance of which we can form but a faint conception, though the immense coal deposits unearthed in the present century tell the tale of primeval vegetable growth proportionate in its exuberance to the abundant presence of the acid that formed its food. Further along the stream of time, many scores of thousands of years nearer to the commencement of our written history, when these gigantic ferns had done their work and fixed a large proportion of that carbon into the shape in which it is now utilized, animal existence became possible, and the same conditions that had previously ministered to immense vegetable forms now made possible the elimination of a mammoth bony framework to support the muscular tissues of animals, giant - like even as compared with the elephant of our own day. There is no doubt that the human race appeared upon the earth just as soon as human respiration became possible, neither can there be any doubt that the " first families " lived in what was a genuine " Garden of Eden " when compared with the more sparse vegetation of the present epoch, or that the peculiar facility afforded to the formation of carbonate of lime justified the assertion of Holy Writ, that "There were giants in those days."

The abstraction of carbonic acid gas from the atmosphere is still progressing, though not so rapidly as in the days of yore. Its appropriation by the vitalized forms that exist upon the land surface is not a permanent loss, as all thus taken away from the general fund by the one, is restored by the compensating activities of another, or yielded up in the disintegration that follows the death of organic forms. But it is not so with life in the sea. The immense quantities of carbonic acid taken up in the secretion of the bony coverings of shell fish, mostly sink to the bottom of the ocean, where they lie forever undisturbed, except when upheaved by a *hypothalassic* volcano. At the immense depths to which they sink there is no wind, no current, but eternal stillness reigns, and not even the play of organic affinities finds room to operate; it is even more than the stillness of death, for there no disintegration follows the departure of the vital principle from its material encasement. The lower coral formations are subject to but little more disturbance.

These fishy processes diminish the amount of carbonic acid in the atmosphere at the rate of about four million tons per century. The process is, however, counteracted to some extent by the tremendous activity of manufacturing fires within the past few years. Indeed, it is not improbable that the last named process will yet attain to such a magnitude as to form an effectual counterbalance to the secretory powers in the restoration of carbonic acid, though the compensation may not be effected without a decrease in the relative proportion of free oxygen in the atmosphere.

We see, then, that the Northwestern conflagrations have carried us back to nearly the same atmospheric conditions as those which existed three centuries ago. And this brings out another important thought. We see that in the history of the past, the elimination of carbonic acid from the atmosphere has been accompanied by a gradual development of animal life, and an equally gradual retrocession of vegetable abundance. While the vegetable kingdom is less royal in its proportions than in the Carboniferous era, the immense interval between then and now has witnessed the upgrowth of all the animal orders above the reptilian, and the successive development of the highest order — man — from a state of savage ignorance to one of high intellectual culture and moral accountability. Knowing, as we do, the intimate physiological connection of the mental with the physical, in man's nature, and the almost abject dependence of that physical nature upon its surrounding conditions — except those of temperature — we can scarcely resist the thought that the progress of the race towards the highest limit of perfection attainable by humanity, has been retarded not less than three centuries, while we estimate that the commercial status of the city of Chicago has been set back barely four years, by the Great Conflagration.

Still another and even more startling idea suggests itself in this connection. What if these fires should be but one of a series of events, designed by the Great Ruler of the Universe, to prevent man from progressing too fast, or too far, in his forward march towards the perfection of knowledge, and of that power which knowledge confers upon its possessor? Our study of the history of the past teaches us nothing more forcibly than this one fact : that all the nations whose records grace prominently the historical page down to a few centuries ago, have reached an *ultimus* beyond which they could not pass, and have relapsed from that point into insignificance as powers and barbarism as peoples. Whether it were the red hand of war, the plague-spot, a change in the beaten track of commerce, or the upgrowth of a luxurious indolence that gnawed out the vitals of the nation, some cause has always operated to break down the power and even the intelligence of peoples. And the records of history show that this grand reversal has occurred at least twice all over the civilized world, while the analogies of reasoning tend to the same conclusion, with geological deductions, that the world as a whole is not exempt from the providential visitation which sweeps out of existence the accumulated learning as well as the treasures of the past, and leaves the race to begin again at the foot of the ladder up which it had toiled so painfully before. If we may be allowed to represent absolute perfection by the rectilineal asymptote of the hyperbola, then the curve may be assumed as the path of humanity towards that perfection. If undisturbed the motion along the curve would never meet the line. But even this motion is not permitted to poor humanity, which, like the comet that attempts to describe the hyperbolic course, is ever and anon subject to perturbations that destroy the old orbit and force the wanderer to seek out a new path in the regions of space.

And, so, it is not impossible, that while the occurrence of the Northwestern fires has furnished to the atmosphere a superabundance of carbonic acid that will stimulate the vegetable world to increased activity to supply the place of that destroyed, the animal creation will retrogress, and man may fall back into the mental conditions of the Reformation period and reproduce the then exceptional intellectual splendors of Bacon and Shakespeare.

A recollection of the fact that large quantities of carbonic acid gas were generated by the fire, will enable us to understand how very many individuals dropped down dead near the scenes of the conflagration, and were afterwards found without the least trace of fire upon the clothing or person. We have already stated that eight per cent. of this gas in the atmosphere is fatal to life. It would be generated in fully this proportion in the neighborhood of the flames, and would thence spread slowly through the air over the whole surface of the earth. The amount of carbonic acid gas evolved by these fires would suffice to saturate the air in the locality to the height of nearly fifty yards from the ground.

But other and very important chemical changes were involved in these wide-spread conflagrations. Everyone has read, if he did not himself pass through the horrible experience, how the very air itself seemed full of fire, how the flames seemed to take giant leaps of many hundreds of yards, breaking out in points far away from the scenes of the general disaster, and how huge balloon masses of flame swept through the sky, to descend and break like a burning (water) spout, licking up every vestige of human life and labor from open clearings to which many had fled as to a haven of safety. These undoubted facts have been ascribed to "electricity"—the agent to which every mystery is generally referred when we fail to assign any other cause. It is true that electric forces were vividly at work during that terrible turmoil of the elements; for we know that no chemical change can occur without the evolution of electrical energy. But the electricity, itself, was only a phenomenon, resulting from the formation of other chemical compounds than the one above referred to.

Immense quantities of water were licked up by the flames, both in city and country, and converted into superheated vapor. At this point the chemical affinities of its constituent gases for each other were overcome by the omnipresent carbon, three pounds of which combined with every pound weight of hydrogen to form what is known as light carburetted hydrogen, while the released oxygen combined with other portions of carbon to form carbonic acid. This carburetted hydrogen is the terror of the coal miner, forming explosive mixtures with the ordinary air of the coal pit. It is also known as marsh gas, being produced by the putrefaction of vegetable matter under water and mud. The volume of this gas was largely supplemented in the city by the coal gas that escaped from the retorts and the supply pipes. This was the material that, mingling with the ordinary air, changed it into a perfect atmosphere of fire, through which the intangible flames could leap, like the lightning flash, from one point to another far distant. Here was the substance of those mysterious balloon masses; they were aggregations of this gas which could not burn where they originated, owing to a lack of oxygen, which had been already sucked out from the air by the incandescent carbon. These masses swept along till they met with a sufficient quantity of fresh oxygen to satisfy their inanimate craving to be reduced back to carbonic acid and water. That condition fulfilled, the change was at once effected, and in the process the devastating flames were kindled afresh in hundreds of places so far removed from the previous locality of the fire that it seemed as if the havoc could only have been wrought by the torch of the destroying angel.

And this hydrogenated atmosphere ministered to the further spread of the devouring element in still another way. The millions of blazing fire-brands that were borne mechanically on the wings of the gale would have died out in an ordinary condition of the atmosphere, before they fell. But after the fire had divorced large quantities of hydrogen from its aqueous matrimony, these brands met with fresh fuel in every yard of their course, and set on fire the hydrogen through which they passed, giving rise to lurid lines of light that resembled the path of a mammoth ærolite. Hence they bore the death warrant to thousands of structures that would have escaped if they had been evolved by a fire of ordinary magnitude. The burning missiles that fell thick and fast on the crib, two miles out in the lake, proved that they had come through an atmosphere highly charged with carburetted hydrogen.

Space will not permit a notice of all the chemical derangements produced by these fires. Among the more important of those not already mentioned is the formation of considerable quantities of ammonia, by the union of portions of this liberated hydrogen with the highly heated nitrogen of the atmosphere. Much of this ammonia will return to the soil to stimulate the growth of vegetable matter, and repair the waste. But no inconsiderable percentage of the whole united with carbon, to form the carbonates of ammonia, or became oxygenated, more slowly, evolving an abundance of nitric acid. The latter gave rise to the peculiar odor experienced after the fire, which was remarked by many as identical with that noticed after a severe thunder storm, and is now known to be due to the formation of nitric acid in the air.

The relative powers of the atomic and molecular affinities vary with a change in temperature — a fact which the writer discussed, two years ago, at considerable length, as revealing to us a glimpse of the constitution of matter. The chemist takes advantage of this, and fire has always been his most efficient aid in working out his transformations of material substantives. Here we have the same agent operating on a gigantic scale, in the great laboratory of Nature, and working out results, the magnitude of which are almost too vast for contemplation. But this power acted equally in obedience to natural law when raging over hundreds of miles, as when manipulated in the chemist's furnace, and assumed the function of teacher even while laughing to scorn the puny efforts of man to control it. The fire has really taught us many valuable lessons, and not the least useful of these to our future welfare, is that conveying a knowledge of wonderful chemical changes, which when in progress perchance excited to wonder the far off inhabitants of the planets Venus and Mars.

We may refer briefly to the more local, but still extensive, effects of the fire, upon the meteorological conditions of the country devastated. It has long been regarded as axiomatic that the destruction of timber and the cultivation of the soil diminish the annual rain supply, and also produce changes in the temperature. This is not wholly true. The ploughing of the ground undoubtedly lessens the amount of water that drains into the rivers, but it is only because the loosening of the soil permits a greater proportion of the rainfall to soak in, instead of running off to feed the water courses. There is, however, the best of reason to believe that the presence or absence of trees has a great deal to do with the quantity of water that falls from the clouds, and so much that we may expect the denudation of so much timber land to be marked by a diminution of not less than two inches, or seven per cent. of the annual rainfall over a large section of the Northwest, while the yearly range of temperature will be widened fully five degrees, the thermometer registering two or three degrees higher in summer and lower in winter than heretofore.

We have already referred to the probability that these fires were part of a section in the Providential plan of earth government. While we cannot accept the doctrine that they were sent either as a punishment to the people of one section, or as a benefit to those of another, we must recognize them as links in the great chain of events, each of which is an effect of some cause, and a producing cause of some subsequent effect. And the same philosophy teaches us that no effect can be greater than its cause, or combined causes. Hence it is absurd to look to the mere upsetting of a kerosene lamp in the city, or the emptying of burning tobacco from a laborer's pipe in the woods, as the efficient causes of these wide-spread disasters. These were the mere incitements — like the knocking of a chip from the shoulders of a man who is spoiling for a fight.

That Chicago was "favorably" situated and constructed for just such a fire, none will deny who remember what she presented — a four-mile line of wooden buildings directly along the path of the southwest gale so common in this region. But the forests *per se*, presented no more unfavorable conditions than in years past; yet they, too, were licked up by the all-devouring flames.

The proximate cause of the conflagrations is found in the fact that the country was unusually dry. One and a half inches of rain fell in Chicago on the 3d of July, but from that date to the time of the fire, on the 9th of October, only two and a half inches fell, whereas the quantity falling in that time had averaged eight and three quarter inches in former years. The rainfall of the summer season was only twenty-eight and one-half per cent. of the average in Chicago; while in the lumber districts it was fully twenty per cent. less than even this parsimonious allowance from the clouds. Meanwhile a hot summer's sun had dried out every particle of the "water of crystallization," as the chemists will perhaps pardon us for calling it, and left the whole as dry as so much tinder. All that it wanted was an *opportunity* to burn, and that want was soon supplied. Thenceforward the fire and the gale had free course, "with none to let or hinder."

But this was evidently only a proximate cause. There was some other cause antecedent to this; we are long past the day when storms of wind or rain are regarded as mere accidents.

If the reader preserves an unburned copy of THE LAKESIDE, August, 1870, he (or she) will find the cause set forth in an article headed "Sun Spots, and their Lessons." In that article we gave the following as the consequences of the obscuration of a large part of the sun's visible surface by dark spots, which have been fully as numerous in 1871 as at the time that sketch was written:

First — A reduction of two degrees in the amount of heat supplied to the earth by the sun (to the whole globe of atmosphere, water, and land,) corresponding to the lessened area of calorifying sun surface. Second — A diminution in the amount of water taken up by the sun from ocean and land (principally from the sea), owing to the diminished evaporating power of the sun; and a decrease of fully four inches in the annual rainfall. Third — Greater sensible heat at many points on the land surface, and a very irregular register of temperature; because a large proportion of the heat supplied by the sun is rendered latent by the evaporation of the water that falls as rain upon the earth's surface. Fourth — An increase in the amount of chemical activity, both in combination and decomposition, a greater display of electric and magnetic phenomena (hence unusual irregularities in temperature); a more rapid growth of vegetation (but) partial crop failures, etc.

These articles were widely copied into the journals of the United States and of Europe, and received marked attention from the scientific men of the day. That every one of the deductions then made was accurately verified, not only in Chicago but all over the world, is now matter of history. Of course, local peculiarities of position, etc., caused many variations from the average; but, as applied to the whole globe, the theory has precisely agreed with the facts. There can be no doubt, therefore, that the very strongly marked deviations from the average rainfall, both the general deficiency and the excessive floods in some localities, have their general cause in the fact that a greater portion of the sun's disk has been obscured by black spots during 1870 and a part of 1871, than at any other time for a hundred years past.

The black patches on the face of the sun, too remote to be visible without the aid of a telescope, though sometimes covering several milions of square miles of its surface, have for some years been recognized by meterologists as potential in producing magnetic storms and auroral displays on the earth. It is but a step further in the same reasoning process to arrive at a point where we can look upon them as causes of greater change in the meteorological conditions of our earth, and as in fluencing materially those circumstances on which its inhabitants depend for the conservation of the order of things under which they live and move.

Elias Colbert.

POLITICAL ECONOMY OF THE FIRE.

WE have space for only one set of economic considerations, that of the distribution of losses; and over this narrow field we must pass rapidly.

It is desirable to have some accurate estimate of the amount of loss in property burned up; but we must content ourselves for the present with an approximate estimate — perhaps we shall never have severely accurate tables; and for the purposes of this paper no figures are required. We omit our own calculations, remarking that the tables already published are a new proof that hyperbole is the favorite figure in the rhetoric of this great people.

The loss sustained by the destruction of houses, stores, machinery, goods, etc., is a *dead* loss; that is to say, it is labor consumed which must be replaced by other labor. In other words, this property must be restored by labor which would have been devoted to the production of new property. All the kinds of property enumerated were surplus earnings of industry, and other surplus earnings of industry must fill the place made empty.

The truth of this statement is disguised by the fact that there are losses not yet mentioned, which are in fact compensated by the beneficence of natural laws; such as rental values of houses burned, and other losses which are mere transfers of property. The burning of a bank - note is of the last character. The bank is so much richer, and the last holder of the note is so much poorer. Society at large is not a loser to the amount of one cent. Treasury notes burned in the Custom House are not even a loss of this personal character; for there is no transfer. The fire did for the Government what a prudent man does for himself when his notes come into his possession.

There are still other losses which are something worse than a dead loss; such are the public records, the scientific collections, the choice books, pictures, and heirlooms.

We confine our view, for obvious reasons, to that part of our losses, the smaller part probably, which has direct and plain relations with production, which can be replaced only by labor subtracted from advancing accumulation.

How else can it be replaced? Were the mechanics who rebuild our houses unemployed? Were there no uses for the lumber, iron, stone, brick, which compose the new city? It is believed that the proportion of unemployed labor and of unused materials is too small to be seriously considered. The apparent gain at these points is greater in appearance because we easily forget all the loss of activity in building in other cities and villages. Such labor as enters into houses has not been a drug in this country for a long time, and there was no reason to apprehend a glut of it when this calamity came. The rebuilding of Chicago will partially arrest building over a wide area, and the labor expended here to repair this loss will be subtracted from other production all over the nation.

Some minds, incapable of general observation, are struck by the concentration of industry upon one point; by the impetus given to those kinds of production which go to fill this fire - made void. But if there be no real loss, if the concentration be really new energy set going by the calamity, the matter ought to be capable of practical illustration. Burn down Mr. Smith's mill, and you will see, if Mr. Smith be enterprising, the same new activity about the ruins of the mill. But Mr. Smith knows perfectly well that he loses whatever it costs him to restore his mill to its former condition. He really loses more; that is, the net earnings of his mill during the time occupied in rebuilding. In Chicago, I have supposed that *this* loss may be compensated in various ways; but it is a piece of mental weakness to deny that what is true in detail is true in general, that what belongs to each of the parts belongs to the whole.

The fire creates a vacuum which is filled by the inflow of surplus earnings of labor from other portions of the country, and the general level of wealth is by just so much reduced.

This loss is very cunningly distributed by natural laws, or their resultant, the machinery of civilization. In such a society as ours, no man's dead losses can be altogether his own. Taxes of many sorts will be shifted from him to others, and in most cases his neighbors will suffer even more directly.

In so far as a fire loss is covered by insurance, it has been distributed in advance by a very fine piece of social machinery. Fire insurance is one of the best implements of a thriftful civilization. It diminishes the shock of a great loss by diffusing it through a large body; it makes individual losses public ones by applying to their cure a cunning system of taxation. Fire insurance is not yet so perfected that *all* its obvious utilities are realized in such a case as the Chicago fire presents. It shares with other beneficent institutions in defects caused by the moral disorders of the world and the imperfect enlightenment of mankind.

In our case, too, especially humiliating defects of system and detail have been developed by our calamity. But it is no light thing that nearly one-fifth of our dead loss is taken up and distributed by the instrument called insurance. No other human contrivance does so much for us; and none performs its labor with so little strain upon the general welfare. Accumulations set apart for this very purpose furnish in most cases the sums paid to policy-holders, and large sums are drawn from England, so widely does insurance distribution range over the field of production. In a good system of insurance, a loss, however large, would draw upon accumulations. Distribution of losses by drafts upon current industry robs insurance of its chief value to society, and discounts its value to the sufferers by fire. For, to whatever extent such distribution disorders trade and industry, or puts strain upon them, he who receives the compensation receives less than his contract calls for — is involved in a general distress produced by the effort to relieve him and others. The large losses of a large fire — in so far as they can be provided for by a good system of insurance — ought to be covered by the sale of public evidences of indebtedness which have a steady value in the markets of the world, wherein the unexpected sale of a few millions of this kind of property involves no general confusion.

Some excuse for current failures is found in the indorsement given by public opinion to other and less safe systems; but it ought not to be possible to plead again that a *great* fire is very unusual. Insurance may just as well be sound, safe, and faithful to its engagements; nothing but a sprinkling of good sense is needed in the premises.

A much less pleasant form of distribution of such a loss as that caused by the Chicago fire is effected by *credit*. The ruined men are those who were in debt, and their creditors, scattered over a wide area, become victims of the catastrophe in Chicago. It is hoped that the catalogue of ruined men is a short one; but a good many will probably escape ruin by compounding with alarmed creditors. It would be a strange phenomenon if there were few men easy enough of conscience to maintain themselves in their old places by drafts upon the fears of their creditors. Instances of this artifice have become so common in some branches of trade as to discredit the trade itself.

In these cases the settlements are made so privately — secrecy being on one side a necessary part of the contract — that the nearest neighbors of the defaulting merchant never hear of the failure. Many a dry goods merchant pursues his trade for years, living in the best style of his town, leading in his church and in local benevolence, whose flowing phylacteries are kept in ample spread by periodical settlements, of a most private character, at New York or Chicago, of accumulated debts for goods, at rates varying from twenty-five to fifty cents upon the dollar. It is probable that Chicago business morality — good according to the standards of the time — has not been found free from the stain of these shameful proceedings.

In other cases, creditors suffer losses with no diminution of honor to the debtor. He cannot pay, he has business ability and is a capitally good customer. Delays of payment enable him to proceed, and the creditor professes in all good form and all sincerity not to lose because he hopes to be paid; but he in reality parts with a portion of his capital to another man upon whose success in a new business the hope of repayment rests. It is a loan, and therefore honorable; it is a forced loan, compelled by certain business amenities, made at a direct and certain disadvantage, and therefore a loss borne, however cheerfully, by the creditor. All unexpected credits for new goods come under the same rule. The Eastern merchants impair their own facilities and means in order to maintain some of their Chicago customers. All points considered, this incident is creditable to trade in general; it refutes some theories of the hardening effects of commercial life upon human nature.

There are other forms of credit distribution which might, in a longer article, deserve special mention. The foregoing may render probably approximate our conjecture that ten millions of the Chicago losses are through credit shifted from the shoulders of direct sufferers by the fire.

It is in place to observe that in so far as capital is brought from abroad into Chicago, either in the form of goods or money, this *transfer* of capital is a means not only of distributing certain per cents of dead loss, but also for putting off for the time being the perception or realizing of loss at this point. This is of very great importance, because it is likely to disguise to ourselves the share which remains for us to bear. By new profits and savings we shall gradually extinguish these new debts, and by distributing our payments lose consciousness of our losses. The men who borrow and pay will not be deceived; but the delightful being who revels in "general aspects" will duly report his impression that there has been no loss whatever, because the brave shows of prosperity go on — upon borrowed capital. Now it is no light thing, no small credit to civilization, that it is possible to distribute in this mode the losses of Chicago, those which remain for Chicago to pay. It is well too that Chicago has such munificence of opportunity and such energy of character, that she can pay large interests and principal too. *" We want only time,"* on the lips of our business men, means much in its personal sense, more still in the deeper and wider significance which makes us believe it. An immense capital lies in the opportunities which open before us and the experience which we bring to our new work.

Still, it cannot come to good that we in any way disguise from ourselves that when all deductions are made a large per cent. of our loss falls on ourselves. Happy for us that we can pay it gradually; that credit tides us over the shoals and provides us with means to use our great advantages.

Charity has also proved in this instance a great distributor of losses. Its field is mainly that area of loss upon which we do not now venture: the rental values and the wages or profits of suspended industry. But Charity has turned political economist in this instance, and to some extent acts upon the area of dead loss.

The comfort of her laborers has been a just pride of Chicago. It was to be expected that the large hearts and clear heads of the Relief Committee should instinctively recur to that condition of health, independence, and hopefulness, which had been so marked a feature of humble life among us.

It seemed an inspiration of genius to seize the occasion to make Charity extend her healing offices in the direction of this same independent condition of labor. It was at once the cheapest charity and the wisest public economy, to aid the poor to rebuild some of those humble homes which in Chicago stand in the place of the tenement barracks of older cities. And to such extent as these restorations are promoted by the Relief Committee, Charity distributes the dead loss of this calamity over the world. Among the millions, this item will seem small in arithmetic; but is very large in its relations to future production. A million of dollars so invested would be the banner million in a record of profits made up ten years from now. It will save families from pauperism and crime, and make them producers and consumers. It saves taxation, reduces claims upon benevolence, recreates workmen, makes markets for goods, and maintains a system of artisan life which is the most hopeful in the world.

We believe that the Relief Committee has never advocated any of the patent nostrums for curing labor of poverty and other wrongs; but it has in this movement done the one only scientific thing to be done in the premises. The laborer's best hold on good wages is in *habits of comfortable living*. To promote that, is worth more than a volume of eight-hour statutes, or a prairie full of international-labor-reform conventions.

It is too much forgotten that cost of production enters into the labor problem in an imperial form. The cost of maintaining laborers, as well as of growing them, is altogether a question of the modes and habits of living prevailing among the humble classes of a country. Wherever laborers are "raised" and subsist upon potatoes and cold water, labor will receive low wages; wages will certainly be higher whenever beef and coffee are substituted for potatoes. A laborer who grew in a straw-covered hovel, or one corner of a basement, and is growing a family in the same style, cannot be well paid. Nor can he be ill paid if he live in his own house and have a fair appreciation of the decencies of life. It works in two ways. The laborer can endure loss of a day now and then — perhaps has a bit of garden upon which he can lay out such a day — and such a laborer cannot be put upon any labor market for less money than good wages. It costs, to produce him, the capital for high rate of wages, and it would cost that to supply his place.

Absentee ownership is also to some extent a distributor of these losses. The resident of another city who owned property burned in Chicago is in a position somewhat similar to that of a foreign insurance company. The entanglements and all other incidents of his loss fall upon other communities.

The railway companies and all other corporations having non-resident stockholders also distribute losses which fall upon such corporations.

That form of distribution which is called *taxation* ought not to be overlooked. It is operative over the whole nation, in the Custom-House and other public property of the nation; over the State to a less extent, falling with most force upon the county, which is scarcely distinguishable from the city for this purpose. But benefits of an unexpected character result from city and county distribution of loss by taxation. Many suffer no loss and some gain by the fire. Taxation should be so modified as to throw all such losses as are repaired by local taxation upon those who *have* in place of those who *had* property.

These are by no means all the ways in which the loss by our fire is distributed. In the language of "The Nation," " it was not the savings of the people of Chicago only which were destroyed, but the savings of at least as many more, who never come within a thousand miles of it, and with their savings nearly everything that made life sweet. . . . The fortunes of the whole race are being so closely linked together by science that there is nobody, from the hod-carrier up to the millionaire, who may not, any morning, read in the paper news from the uttermost ends of the earth, depriving him of his fortune or his daily bread."

The political economist finds in such facts new reasons for hopefulness and also for apprehension. He is stimulated to increased confidence in the wholesomeness of the natural laws of society, to new fear of the consequences of their disobedience. We cannot forget that bad men, and careless good men, are not restrained from careless handling of great social concernments by the magnitude and range of the perils they thus invite, and when fools abound it is not cheerful to feel that any one of them may put us all to grief by one careless action or one piece of negligence.

The effect of the sudden destruction of a great mart of wealth upon human energy, in increaing or lessening its quantity or determining its direction, cannot be omitted from our survey. In one point of view, it seems probable that loss and gain are in equilibrium. On one side we see men of some years disheartened and retired from productive exertion. On the other, we see places opened for younger men. Assuming that this energy must have taken the same direction, we have only personal and moral reasons for regret. But if we consider that the young men are forced by this event into trade, who would else have been forced into letters, art, science, one perceives in the persistency of the old direction of force an absolute loss and a new danger. For, whatever retards the natural movement to higher forms of energy, whatever arrests the progress of a society to a higher life, gives to the lower order of activities facility for crystallization and lessens the probability of a better life. If in a town composed of huts, an annual fire made it necessary to annually rebuild, the people could only be hut builders and hut-dwellers. If young men are demanded to produce grain and build houses, they cannot frequent colleges, libraries, or art studios. If all the income of Mr. Smith is required to furnish shelter and bread for his family, his daughters will be inadequately educated.

That general condition of social comfort which has been the general aim of our young civilization is in itself a good never to be despised or undervalued. That this fire subtracts in thousands of homes, not in Chicago alone, from this comfortable *status*, is by itself an evil not covered up because patiently borne. But it is a greater evil that, mixed up with these means of comfortable home life, there were accumulations intended for the education of young men and women On a smaller scale the fire repeats the greatest of the burdens of the war by subtracting from the education of a generation.

It is not well for us to be taught in the school of pain, until it is true that we cannot learn in a better school. And therefore one may distrust the social effects of shocks given by this calamity to brave and noble men among us who are silent sufferers at home. One hears every day in soft accents of sympathetic friends, of this and that silver-haired merchant, public servant, or saint, on whose bounty the poor have fed, by whose hands churches have risen out of the ground, through whose wisdom the city has been established on some of its permanent supports, from whom the fire took away not merely goods but all the forces whereby goods grew. Many a prop is gone from under the civilizing institutions that rose somewhat too slowly in Chicago.

It is not merely that these forces are gone, that some of the best of our hands are nerveless, and some of the warmest friends of charitable causes rendered helpless; the very mode of their paralysis is an evil, because sudden and undistributed as by ordinary death or failure in business, and because it has destroyed some of the procreant force of charity. Some celestial color will be missed from our life at the very time when — after the charity of our neighbors has ceased to flow this way — the greatest demand for public spirit will exist with the smallest supply.

It is painful to follow the lines of distribution over which this loss travels out over the land, and to mark everywhere the disproportionate burden thrown upon the nobler uses of life. Whatever educates, as books, newspapers, magazines, higher schools, and churches, suffer out of proportion because material wants are imperious Just because we can hide here such a large proportion of our loss, we shall the sooner recover the shows of our prosperity; but it is a loss — this of education — which has no compensation, and torments the thoughtful spirit with painful apprehensions. The vast army of counter-jumpers, bartenders, and political bummers, is recruited from among the imperfectly educated young men — the young men who have neither book learning nor trades, and want all forms of discipline and culture.

To know a danger is to avoid it. The press and the pulpit have it in their power to greatly decrease the impending evils of diminished benevolence and education. These great lights and forces may, by giving special attention to this danger, prevent the excessive taxation of culture and charity to repair our loss. Of these we must lose much. Let our lamp-bearers see to it that we lose no more than we must.

D. H. Wheeler.

APPENDIX.

CHICAGO AND THE RELIEF COMMITTEE.

"THE Fire," said a distinguished orthodox clergyman of this city in a recent sermon, "has burnt up a good deal of sectarianism in Chicago." Whether this be true or not it is not our purpose to inquire; but it has certainly brought into zealous practice a great deal of unsectarian Christianity. "If," says one of the most vigorous and eloquent writers of our generation, "If it be true Christianity to dive with a passionate charity into the darkest realms of misery and of vice, to irrigate every quarter of the earth with the fertilizing stream of an almost boundless benevolence, and to include all the sections of humanity in the circle of an intense and efficacious sympathy; if it be true Christianity to destroy or weaken the barriers which had separated class from class and nation from nation, to free war from its harshest elements, and to make a consciousness of essential equality and of a genuine fraternity dominate over all accidental differences; * * * if these be the marks of a true and healthy Christianity, then never since the days of the Apostles has it been so vigorous as at present." When these words were written we had not then, as our newspapers so love to say. "passed recently through a disastrous conflagration;" but no more striking illustration of their truth has been, or, let us hope, will be given in our time, than in these last three months of our history. Both in what has been done for us and in what has been done among us, true Christianity has dived here into the darkest recesses of misery; has flowed over us with a fertilizing stream of almost boundless benevolence; and has enfolded us as in an intense and effective sympathy. It is true that Chicago, more than any other city on the globe, is made up of people gathered together from all civilized countries. The oldest native born citizen is only about thirty-five years of age, and there is hardly an old man or an old woman in all its three hundred thousand inhabitants. Much the larger portion of its adults are young, or in the prime of life, and all, or nearly all, have left old homes and kindred elsewhere, to whom they are bound by the closest ties of affection and interest.

The fire broke out on Sunday evening at ten o'clock, and the last house it caught — four miles distant in a straight line from the starting point — was still blazing at eleven o'clock the next night. In that twenty-five hours the news of the disaster was carried across an ocean and a continent, and the hearts of hundreds of thousands were wrung with anxiety and suspense as to the fate, not merely of their fellow creatures, but of parents and children, of brothers and sisters, and of intimate friends. The intense sympathy which was everywhere shown was due, doubtless, in a measure to this deep personal interest in the event; but the contagion of that sympathy ran through every town and city, at home and abroad, as irrepressible and as consuming as the hot flames that were even then leaping from house to house through our doomed streets. The barriers which separate class from class, and nation from nation, were no longer remembered. In London, in Vienna, in Paris, in all European capitals, instant measures for relief followed the first imperfect comprehension of the calamity. It was only necessary to placard upon a wagon in any New York street the one word "Chicago," to bring out from every house its inmates, loaded with whatever of clothing or of food they could lay their hands on, for the succor of a suffering people a thousand miles away. The rich and the poor vied with each other in giving of their abundance or their poverty; and from the western border of the American continent to the eastern boundary of Europe, a chord of tender feeling and Christian charity thrilled through all peoples with pity and with love for those who were thus stricken with sudden poverty, and who looked up hopeless and in despair into the pitiless heavens, red with the reflection of their burning homes.

Of what depths of feeling were stirred many touching evidences were given, in the hundreds of boxes of goods sent here to private persons for distribution. Stores of household treasures that had lain untouched and hidden away from the light of day for many years, too precious from cherished associations to be put to common use, were brought out now, and dedicated, as it were, to a sacred mission. Their character, and the fashion of them, evidently showed, as they were lifted from their places here, what tender memories must have been entwined about them, and how intense the pious devotion was that could enforce consent to part with them now forever. Sheets and blankets and coverlets, and stores of other homely stuff, as precious once to some good housewife as the contents of Mrs. Tulliver's cedar closet were to her, and which some loving daughter had laid away as a legacy too sacred to be put to any common purpose, were sent as a fitting gift to those who sat in the ashes of all past memories. Garments, doubtless the last worn by friends who were dead, and which carried with them some semblance to the "dear flesh" they once covered, were sent where their new use was held to be no profanation of the old, sad associations that belonged to them. Now and then, packed away with unusual care, was some quaint, old-fashioned suit of baby-clothing, or child's dress, which was not parted with, we may be sure, without many tears, for its very age told of a cherished grief in the heart of a loving mother, who, long years ago, had laid a little one to its final rest, and now sanctified that sorrow with the hope that the robes of her baby, who died when she was young, would go to comfort the heart of some other young mother who still clasped a living child to her bosom.

There was no display, and no obtrusion of any feeling of this sort; the only evidence of it was in the mute testimony of the things themselves; but they bore as certain witness as though they spoke with tongues. In the presence of a disaster involving so many in utter ruin, and the immediate deprivation of the bare necessities of life, to hold back anything which could be parted with, seemed to thousands an act of cruel selfishness which no merely private sorrow or personal comfort could palliate; and the world will never know how many sacrifices, very hard to make, were laid upon the altar of that charity, how many crosses were lifted up cheerfully and borne bravely that others' burdens might be lightened. If there was great suffering, so also was there great love; and in the dire disaster that befel Chicago came a swift witness to the truth that far more powerful than any dogma in the minds of men in our time is the law, that " ye help one another."

As the benevolence of the world was without stint and without parallel, so was its confidence boundless. Where there was so much distress, it had to be assumed that of necessity there must be honest men and women who would rob neither the poor nor their friends. Millions were given in money, and hundreds of thousands of dollars' worth in goods. The trust involved in the use of so large an amount of property was enormous, and it was by no means a foolish or an over-anxious question, in the first days after the fire, whether the duties of that trust would be faithfully discharged. Private donations of large value came immediately to private persons in whose integrity and judgment friends at a distance knew they could confide. That confidence, we have no doubt, has been uniformly justified; and we know that many men and women have labored incessantly, though unobtrusively, for the last three months in seeking for and relieving suffering among a class which but for them would have submitted to the very extremity of want. What has been done in this way, and by small voluntary associations of ladies, has not been and never can be told, for they have done good in secret, and have reached cases which no public charity could ever touch. Whether right or wrong, there are many families who shrank far more from any exposure of their poverty than from starvation, and their sensitiveness has been respected by those whose privilege it was to relieve their wants. But the larger class was of those whom public charity must aid or they would perish. Between them and absolute poverty there was, at all times, only the precarious barrier of their daily bread, earned by their daily labor, with some small but indispensable accumulation of household goods; and when these were swept away, they stood face to face with gaunt hunger and blank despair. They stood face to face with them, but only for a day. Had such a calamity as ours occurred to a city of three hundred and fifty thousand people, which was not connected with all the world by telegraphic wires, and which was not a railroad centre, death would have been the portion of very many ere succor could have reached them; but here not even one human creature perished from destitution. The wires and the rails assured us, before the sun had set over the burning city, that none need suffer for food or clothing; and there was none of that desperate despair that might have led to desperate remedies.

There was anxiety enough, and apprehension enough, as everybody remembers, in the first few days, in a city without gas, without water, overworked, sleepless, distracted with cruel rumors, carefully collated by a reckless press, of ruffianism, robbery, and incendiarism; but the real danger of that fearful time seemed to escape attention, or, at least, to find no voice. That danger was whether, after all, the boundless benevolence of the world would avail us anything; whether all those millions of money and all those trains of food and of clothing should ever reach those for whom they were intended, or whether committees should steal and squander all they could lay their hands on, and a hungry and naked mob should divide among the strongest the material in kind of which they knew there would be no just distribution. That we narrowly escaped that peril, there can be no doubt. Political adventurers saw, or thought they saw, their opportunity. Where would Chicago and her wretched people have been to-day, had it been their fate to have remained another week at the mercy of those men, or their like, whom a Grand Jury has since called to the bar of justice to answer for their ordinary method of municipal administration? It was not merely that there was no city government equal to the occasion, but that in the utter corruption of our city politics there would have been even no attempt to meet so terrible an emergency. There would have been a desperate scramble for the spoils, first of officials, and then of the mob; and the disaster of destruction would have been followed by the deeper disaster of disgrace and anarchy.

But one just man can save a city. Fortunately Mayor R. B. Mason controlled officially all the contributions in money and material sent for the relief of the people, and fortunately Mayor Mason was both a man of probity and a man of sense. He saw not only the thing that was not to be done, but he saw also, just as clearly, the thing to do. To a citizens' committee, which had on it some good men, but which was controlled by those who were politicians by trade, and therefore not good, he gave a fair trial of three days. Three days were enough to show that we were going to the bad almost as fast as the fire swept from the West Side to the North, and with a result quite as certain. He looked about him for men who were honest as well as wise; men identified with the true interests and the fair fame of Chicago; men who would not if they could, and could not if they would, betray the sacred trust which the sympathy and the benevolence of the whole Christian world had put into its hands; and he found an organization ready-made, better-fitted for the work to be done than if it had been created at the moment for that special purpose.

On the 12th of October he handed over to The Relief and Aid Society a hundred thousand homeless, hungry, and almost naked people, with the means to house and feed and clothe them, and held the Society before the world, by proclamation, responsible for the gravest duty that ever yet fell upon private citizens in the administration of the largest charity the world has ever known. What special considerations they were that moved the Mayor to this decision, is not of much moment, inasmuch as the result has proved that the decision was a wise one, and nothing is so wise as wisdom. But he doubtless reflected that the men he selected were, from their circumstances, social position, and private character, above personal temptation; that they could have no partisan purpose or political end to gain by the perversion of a public fund; that they had had long experience in dispensing charity to the needy, moved thereto by no other motive than a sense of humane and Christian duty. Their acts, moreover, would be open to public inspection and public criticism, for the Society was a chartered institution, and by its act of incorporation its directors were obliged "to make a report at least once a year to the City Council of Chicago, giving a full account of their doings, a statement of their receipts and expenditures, verified under oath"; and by the same act it is provided that "any officer, agent, or member of said corporation, who shall fraudulently embezzle or appropriate to his own use any of the funds or property of the said corporation, shall be deemed guilty of larceny, and liable to be indicted and punished accordingly."

In accepting the grave responsibility bestowed upon them, the officers of the society gave the strongest guaranty possible, first, in their character and position as private citizens, and, second, in their relation to the law as a public body, that the duties devolving upon them would be discharged wisely, honestly, and humanely. The Mayor could no doubt have selected other citizens quite as wise, quite as honest, and quite as humane, to whom he could have entrusted the care of the army of his indigent constituents to be marshalled into peace and comfort and thrift, but he could not hold them responsible to any legal obligation; or he might have asked of the Legislature the creation of the legal obligation, but then the selection of the citizens would not have been in his hands. The existence of the Relief and Aid Society relieved him of any such dilemma; its officers were the very men he wanted, and they were already answerable for a faithful discharge of the trust they accepted. It was fortunate for Chicago, and fortunate for the Mayor that he saw his way clearly.

It is not details but results that we are considering, for the method and machinery of their labors the Committee have fully explained in their first Special Report, which is within everybody's reach. It is by their fruits that those labors are to be judged, and their method, however admirable as a statement, is good for nothing as a fact if it does not stand this experimental test. We are not, it is proper to state, the advocate of the Society in any partisan sense; we are under no obligation to it even to the value of a daily ration; and we bear no relation to it whatever that can blind our eyes or warp our judgment. Indeed, we observe one notable fact in regard to the Relief Committee,—that they do not defend themselves from any attacks that have been made upon them, nor ask, so far as we know, any defence from anybody else. They are too busy to listen to cavil, though always ready to hear complaints; too much in earnest to stop for idle discussion, though always ready to receive suggestions; too strong in their own integrity and too firmly persuaded of the magnitude of their task and the practical results of their way of handling it, to permit themselves to be turned aside by captious fault-finding. If there are points in their management that need to be explained, the explanation, we presume, will come in due season, and on the whole we think the public can find patience to wait for it. For meanwhile the welfare of Chicago to-day, her reputation the world over, and her character for the future, dating *urbis conflagratio*, are recorded indelibly and unmistakably in the daily lives of a hundred thousand people, whom the Relief Committee have in charge. The problem to be solved in regard to them had three conditions: First, that none of them should perish; second, that none of them should suffer for want of food, or of clothing, or of shelter; and third, that when these points were attained, there should be left, as the grand result, a hundred thousand industrious, thrifty, and happy people, and not a hundred thousand idle, discontented, and helpless paupers. Three months ago, the fire left them all in absolute destitution, and not one of them knew, on the morning of the 9th of October, where they should lay their heads that night, where their next meal was to come from, or wherewithal they should be clothed. But not one human creature has died as a consequence of a destitution so unprecedented; there has been among them no real suffering for the want of the necessaries of life, during a season of unusual severity, and all the hardship that has been endured is positively less than the poor are compelled to submit to in ordinary winters; and not one of all this multitude is left without a home of some sort, and many of them have been put in houses of their own, almost as comfortable and almost as good as those they occupied before the fire swept them away.

To establish a system that would do this, and do it in the shortest possible time, on the very edge of winter, was an enormous work, requiring energy, directed by the most unerring judgment, and commercial ability and experience backed by the most careful economy, and the strictest probity. Nor was it a work of a single day, or week, or month, but of half a year; demanding foresight, the exactest calculation of means to ends, unwearied and constant labor, and keen insight into the character of men to whom the details of the work were entrusted. Commerce, we know, clothes and feeds and houses any given community, whether large or small; but commerce works by precedent, calculates supply by a known or probable demand, whether of necessaries or luxuries, and does its work by many self-appointed agents whose separate sphere is narrow and who easily master the defined limits of their activity. So we know that armies, large and small, are lodged and fed and clothed; but the nucleus of the army is the squad of the recruiting sergeant, and the agglomeration of the parts is not permitted till Quartermasters General and Commissaries General are provided with all that is needed for sustenance and protection. But here was a community for which commerce could make no calculation; of which the law of supply and demand had no cognizance; for whose wants there were no agents, and where every individual member had lost all past accumulations, had no resources from which to provide for the most pressing wants, were suddenly deprived of the ordinary means of subsistence, and stood with outstretched hands, hopeless, destitute, and almost as helpless as when he came into the world. Here was an army, not mustered by squads at the sergeant's convenience, to await the orders of Quartermasters and Commissaries; but an army, a hundred thousand strong, of men, women, and children, huddled together in the extremity of distress and terror, to become marshalled on the instant into an organized body, or left to become a starving, fierce, and lawless mob. We look with pride upon Chicago rising again slowly and laboriously above her two thousand acres of ashes and ruins; but had there been among us no men wise enough and strong enough to take into their hands the essential government of the city, and to dispense with prudence and forethought the largess of the world, we should have still sat mourning in that abomination of desolation.

Perhaps the time has not yet come when it can be definitely pronounced that the third condition of the problem has been fully solved. Pauperism begets pauperism, and the danger always is that it will grow with what it feeds on. But to so care for this impoverished and ruined multitude that they shall neither lose the sense of self-respect and independence nor the habit of self-support, has been from the beginning the aim of the Relief Committee. The very poor are always on the verge of despair, and an event which only serves to nerve the energies of those in better circumstances, sinks them often in hopeless beggary. But fortunately there are almost no very poor in Chicago. Plenty of work and good wages and the chances for the acquisition of property are here so uniform that their influence is marked upon the character of the people. The losses by the fire are counted by the hundreds of millions, but the estimate is made up from the destruction in merchandise and buildings and insurance, visible wealth, the value of which could be easily reckoned. No account is taken of the little unseen accumulations of the poorer class, the household goods, the fruits of long and painful industry, the stores for winter use, the tools and implements of mechanics and laborers, all of small value when considered separately, but large in the aggregate. It is one of the striking facts revealed by the business of Relief that the poor of Chicago are not of the very poor, but that the habit of forehandedness is almost universal among them, and that there were very few who were not losers by the fire of something more than the bare necessities of living from day to day. As an illustration among many, we know of a poor German woman, who, at the wash-tub and over the ironing-board, had accumulated a property of several thousand dollars, and had made the last payment, on Saturday, the 7th of October, on a house costing two thousand dollars, which the fire the next night swept away. She recounts to any listener the story of her labors and her losses, enumerates the comfortable and handsome dresses she had laid by, among other blessings, for her old age, but breaking down invariably when she comes to the fifth, which was trimmed with velvet. Houses and furniture she can speak of with calmness and resignation, but the memory of the velvet trimmings is too much for her. Everywhere, in odd and unexpected ways and places, the evidence of the habit of accumulation crops out and shows how far the spirit of the people is from that of paupers. It was good ground to work upon, and the Relief Committee have cultivated it diligently and well. That work is the rule, and idleness to be tolerated only where enforced by want of work or sickness, is a wholesome regulation, never lost sight of; though it is sometimes necessary to remind some over-zealous visitor, disposed to enforce too rigidly the maxim "that he who will not work neither shall he eat," that Chicago winters were not known in Judea. But applicants for aid do not usually shrink from toil. The old habit speedily resumed its sway; cheerful hopefulness soon took the place of despair when they found that there was help at hand to aid them over slippery places, so putting the past calamity behind them they make a new beginning, aiming at the bright future to which they had always looked with a steady face. Here and there, it is true, imposters turn up, who recount their sufferings and flaunt their rags with pitiful pleadings and wonderful dramatic power. But, by following their doublings from station to station, it is found that one scamp would have attempted twenty frauds where, under a less perfect system, there would have seemed to be twenty rogues.

From the class who really need aid there is no grumbling. They understand the situation and accept it. They comprehend the tremendous difficulties of the work the Committee have in hand; are helpful and not repining; know that they ought not to have, and do not expect to have, anything but temporary help, and strive with all their might to keep pauperism from the door as manfully as ever they fought against hunger. In nothing is this spirit so manifest as in the success of the plan of providing "Shelter houses," the wisest and the most permanent in its effect of any of the measures adopted by the Committee. To feed and to clothe the poor was absolutely necessary, but, after all, was only temporary relief. If nothing more could be done the inevitable consequence would be that many would sink into hopeless despondency, and the town be burdened, in the spring, with a crowd of helpless paupers. The proposition to provide all whose homes had been burned, but who owned or leased the lots on which they stood, with a cheap but comfortable house, was accepted with delight and gratitude. It gave a fixed value at once to what they had left, the land; it provided them with a home of their own; it decreased their expenses by the amount of rent they would have had to pay elsewhere, and left all their earnings for the support of their families; it made them at once self-supporting; it made them again independent citizens, giving them once more the proud sense of being property-holders, of having a share in the well-being of the community, bestowing upon them a renewed incentive to good order, industry, and thrift. Many of these houses the occupants, with little savings of their own, improved and added to, so that they were made almost if not quite as good as those they had lost. A considerable portion of the burnt district is thus already built up and occupied by a permanent population which would otherwise have been scattered or have remained in penury, but which may now be relied upon to furnish mechanics and laborers for the future wants of the city. About six thousand of them have already been built; to these probably two thousand more will be added in the next two or three months, providing homes for not less than forty thousand people. Their cost will be perhaps one-third of the whole of the Relief Fund, but it is money not expended but invested, is a permanent gift to Chicago and that portion of those who lost their all by the fire. The money could have been put to no wiser or more beneficent use, both in its material and its moral influence; and the benefactors, whose generous sympathy made it possible, will feel, when they come to understand its character, that by such a disposition of their bounty far more has been done for Chicago than they ever intended.

We hope that we do not seem to have indulged in superlatives. That spirit of braggadocio which pretended to a boastful pride in the extent of the fire, and vaunts itself now on what it is pleased to assume as an exceptional display of activity since on the part of our business people — as if a man in deep water could do anything but swim or else sink to the bottom — that boastful tendency commends itself neither to good taste nor sound judgment. But the fire was certainly a remarkable event, and it has had some consequences which the political economist and the moralist may consider with profit. "You have had," said the young Russian prince, who was here a few days since, "you have had a great burn." This may be stated as a fact without offending anybody's most delicate sense of modesty. It certainly was, at least, "a great burn" that destroyed between fifteen and sixteen thousand buildings; burnt over more than two thousand acres of a populous city; raged steadily for five and twenty hours unchecked and uncontrolled, even for a single moment, and turned out into the night probably a hundred and twenty-five thousand people, stripped, to the scanty clothing in which they ran for their lives, of all their earthly possessions. It needs no expletives to describe it. The most vivid imagination and the most ingenious invention halt lamely and tamely far behind its mingled facts of tragedy and comedy. For here were a siege and a battle; a defeated army and a flying host; the terrors of a famine and a revolution; — and here were the grim humor of despair; the ludicrous display, in thousands of ways, of personal peculiarities and eccentricities surprised into sudden betrayal; the unreservedness and frankness of the simple human relation where conventionalism and artificial restraint came out in curious and absurd contrast with a state of nature. But more remarkable than the fire itself are the events that have followed it. Cities have been burned down before, and battles and sieges, and the flight of multitudes, and revolutions and famines, are scattered thick through all the pages of history. But nowhere ever before has it been recorded that the terror and desolation and destitution which mark such events have passed away and not a single human life, after the first shock and struggle, has been lost; not one has endured the pangs of hunger or of cold; not one is left without a shelter; not one act of violence or of open immorality has followed the sudden change from settled life to the severing of so many social ties dependent upon it; but that, on the contrary, the terrible ordeal has been passed through in safety. That is, we mean, aside from the inevitable losses and distress which come as by the act of God and cannot be avoided, none of the ordinary results of great calamities have followed here, among that class who became peculiarly the care of public charity, and about whom alone the world is entitled to know. Disaster overwhelmed them, but they have not sunk; sudden poverty, like a thief in the night, came upon them, but none are sick, or starving, or in prison; they have looked a future in the face that was all darkness, but have not despaired; the wrath of God seemed to many to have been visited upon them, and yet they lost no faith. These facts are patent to whomsoever will take the trouble to inform himself of that condition of Chicago that lies beneath the surface; and it is not an inconsiderate eulogy upon the Relief and Aid Committee to ascribe this unprecedented condition of things, following a great public calamity, to the wisdom, the self-devotion, and the courage with which they have discharged the duties of the great and sublime trust that fell into their hands. If we are right in believing that here is a new phenomenon in the history of civilization, then we do not err in commending it to the consideration of thoughtful men.

Sydney Howard Gay.

Printed in Dunstable, United Kingdom